So Be It!

MY WARTIME SERVICE IN THE ROYAL AIR FORCE

November 1938 to February 1946

DON SUTHERLAND

IN MEMORY OF OLD FRIENDS AND THEIR COMRADESHIP, FRIENDSHIP AND LOYALTY.

GOD BLESS THEM ALL!

Contents

EDITOR'S NOTE

Don Sutherland first contacted me in March 2011 in response to an online request for any information from groundcrew who had worked on the Blackburn Skua dive-bomber. He was good enough to send me his memories of working on that aircraft. Then in 2012 I received a copy of Don's memoir of his complete service in the RAF via his daughter Janet Martin. Although written for his family I found it a fascinating document. At the time I told Don that it needed wider circulation. Sadly, Don died in July 2013. Retirement gave me the opportunity to edit the document to make it more suitable for that larger audience. The original document was dictated by Don and retained a distinct feel of someone telling their story over a pint in their local pub. However, it was difficult to follow at times. I have tried to make it more readable without losing too much of the "feel" of the original. I make no apologies for a certain amount of bad grammar; I feel it is necessary to retain Don's "voice". I have added footnotes to give background to the events described and put them in context. I only wish Don had lived to share in my research. I would have loved to tell him the background story of the aircraft crash he braved to recover the body of a crewman and that the Doctor who attended to him after his horrific accident went on to found the Paralympic movement. But perhaps most of all I would like to have told him that those aircraft he dutifully pulled fuel bowsers to, and ferried crews to, were a crucial part of winning the Battle of the Atlantic.

There are lots of accounts of the RAF in World War Two written by officers but precious few by the "other ranks" (those that do exist are often just a series of anecdotes). Don's story is remarkably frank. He does not paint himself as a hero or put a gloss on events. His remarkable memory, without the aid of diary or flying logbook, sheds a light into the daily lives of the ground crews in those desperate days.

JW Dell, 2018.

FOREWORD

Don Sutherland – my father. When he started writing his memoirs he was in his 80's, retired and needed a hobby. I bought him a computer and he soon mastered it, even downloading pictures and including them in his stories. He started writing short articles about his life in the RAF during WWII before embarking on 'So Be It'.

Don was born in Birkenhead, Cheshire on the Wirral Peninsula on 26 July 1921. He was the eldest of five children.

Don left school at the age of 14 and went out to work. When he turned 16 he became an apprentice joiner at Cammel Lairds Shipyard. He signed up for the Royal Air Force shortly after his 17th birthday.

In 1946 Don returned to his home in Rock Ferry, Birkenhead and lived there with his wife Rita and baby Graham working once again at the Birkenhead Docks. They moved down to Portsmouth after a couple of years and lived in Southsea (Rita's home town). I was born there and my younger brother Malcolm, five years later.

In 1958 Don, Rita and the three children left Britain to live in New Zealand. Don's parents, a brother and a sister had been living there for 5 years and were well established.

During the six weeks on board the SS Southern Cross Don kept himself occupied. He formed a musical group and was on the entertainment committee, assisting with the organisation of social events and deck sports, etc.

Once in New Zealand Don was immediately employed as a carpenter and they soon settled into the New Zealand way of life. He became involved in several organisations; the Air Force Association, the RSA and the Savage Club (entertainment club) where he met up with 3 other men and formed a musical group.

Don was forced to give up carpentry work as a result of his accident on the airfield in 1943 and found alternative employment. It was while Don and Rita were managing the student shop at a university Don coached and managed the football team.

They moved to a small town in the centre of the North Island in the 1970's and opened a corner shop. They spent a very busy few years there and soon became used to the small-town way of life. Don had joined the local brass band as a drummer and when a movie was being filmed nearby he played a small part. He certainly experienced variety in his life.

They sold the business in 1985 and returned to the UK for a visit for the first time since moving to New Zealand. On their return they sold their house. They moved again and lived comfortably and happily for several years until Don's health deteriorated and they moved into care.

Don lived a long and very fulfilled life, was never bored, always cheerful and had a wonderful sense of humour. It was a regular sight when visiting him in his room at the rest home to see him surrounded by staff members listening to his jokes.

Don passed away aged 92 in 2013. His busy heart had worn out. So be it.

Janet

MAP OF MAINLAND UK SHOWING SOME OF THE PLACES MENTIONED.

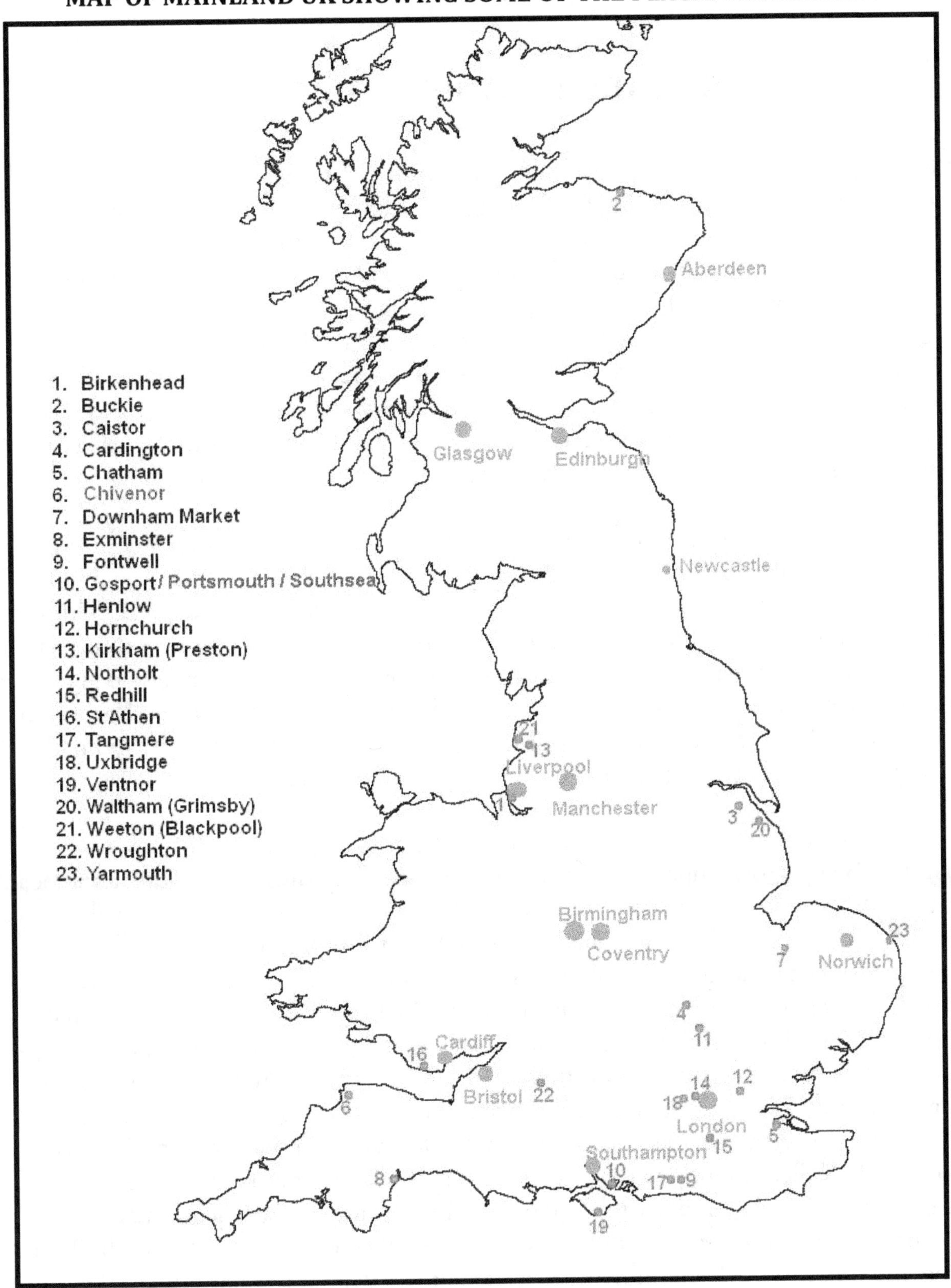

SKYWARD (NOV 1938 - SEPT 1939)

Being employed as an apprentice joiner in Cammell Lairds shipyard at Birkenhead had its advantages, but also its disadvantages. Following the launch of the Mauritania on July 28th 1938, two days after my 17th birthday, our workload had eased off to such an extent that I found myself not so much bored, as restless. Having lived a life of outside activity, including having a paper round from when only nine years old, my being tied to the workbench day in and day out was beginning to create an inner tension. By way of relaxation, my mate Val and I would shoot off up town during our one-hour lunch break. It was on the day Val decided to visit the barber and have his locks trimmed not far from the famous Argyle Theatre, that I decided to walk on and do some window shopping.

To my surprise, one shop that had closed down was now a recruiting centre for the RAF. The information and display of photos in the window were most interesting; to such an extent I didn't hesitate to march in and have a chat with the Sergeant. He was quite handsome and had a friendly manner. The next thing you know, I had arranged to sit an exam and questionnaire and have my doctor give me a fitness test. Val, being somewhat of the excitable type, beamed when I told him what I had done. "Sounds fantastic" he cried "but what will your mam and dad have to say?" "That will be problem number one." I replied.

It was a matter of two to three days before I got the message across to my parents. Being grown-ups, they could see the possibility of another war in the near future. "If you stay where you are," said Dad, "you won't be called up for the army." "I appreciate that," I replied, "but look at it this way, if a war does eventually come I would not only be prepared but in the RAF and not in the Army." I then added for the benefit of Mam, "Just think, you won't have to feed me or pay out for clothes. Plus, the fact I will be making an allotment in your name." I think it was then I won the battle. On Saturday of the following week I made my appearance at the recruiting office, armed with my doctor's certificate. "Well that's a start," beamed the Sergeant, "but it will be a matter of time before you will be called upon for your written test and questionnaire." He went on to explain how it takes time for those in authority to study my application and medical information. It was now a matter of patience on my part, for I felt like a dog straining on the lead. Shortly after, by coincidence, when standing in the doorway of the dry cleaners after closing hours and yacking to my mates, we witnessed searchlights endeavouring to locate an aircraft. "Looks as if another war is expected," piped up one of the know-alls, "and by the way that feller Hitler is performing it won't surprise me." I had yet to let the cat out of the bag, so to speak, for had they been aware of my intentions to enrol, I would have been left wide open to being lectured. Eventually I received notification to report for the aptitude test. It was a Saturday morning at 10 a.m. I arrived on the dot, was led upstairs and sat down at a desk. "If you have any problems," said the sergeant, "just shout down and I will come up to help you out." The first paper was fairly straightforward, wanting information regarding my date of birth, the school I attended, and the type of employment I had been engaged in. The test paper wasn't so straightforward and required a fair amount of brain work. It was at this point in time, when endeavouring to concentrate, that the Sergeant below started singing at the top of his voice. One had to admit he had a fantastic voice and he was confident with the lyrics. I found out later the song was the hit of the day and recorded by "The Andrew Sisters", called *Bei Mir Bist Du Schoen.*

From where I was sitting, it sounded like *"By mere bister shane please let me explain".* My interpretation was *"My dear Mister Shane you are something of a pain."* To ease my tension, I lit another cig and inhaled deeply. Having done the best I could, I called to him downstairs and he was up in a flash. The next few moments were spent in silence, allowing him time to browse my effort. "You've done well," he said, in a voice somewhat lower than earlier, "I can now get them off in the post on Monday." He then warned me to have patience as it could be some time before I heard from them. "You must remember," he added, "you will not be the only one enrolling so it will be a case of arranging a time and date to suit all concerned."

I was kept waiting so long I was beginning to think I had been turned down. It was not until 10th November when I received orders to see the Sergeant who was to explain when and where I will be on my way. As it was Remembrance Day the following day it was left to the next day for my reporting as required. The Sergeant read out the instructions then gave me a copy. On Friday the 25th November I was to report to a Sergeant on the platform at Lime Street Station in Liverpool, at 9 . 30 a.m.

This arrangement enabled me to work out my week's notice and left a few days to prepare for my departure. Somewhere along the line our mam came up with an old suitcase and proceeded to fill it with a change of underwear etc. I did not require shaving equipment, owing to the fact I had yet to reach that stage! On the Friday morning our dad had me up and about before he departed for work. He shook me by the hand, wished me all the luck and dashed out to catch the bus. As to be expected, Mum was more emotional so I was glad to be on my way. So be it!

Having had luck with transport; bus, ferry and the tram, I arrived 15 minutes early and had no trouble locating the Sergeant on the middle of a near empty platform and armed with his clip-board. He greeted me with a firm handshake when accepting the copy of my instructions. "Hopefully the other four will be on time," he said with a half‑smile, "the train won't wait for latecomers." No sooner had he spoken than two more arrived with the other two close behind. "Thank God for that," he muttered, heaving a sigh.

In next to no time we entered the carriage nearby and had hardly become settled when the whistle blew and we were on our way.

For quite some time the atmosphere was akin to that of doctor's waiting room. I expect that like myself, they would be wondering if they had done the right thing. It wasn't like going from one job to another whilst still on home ground, for this move was totally different and we would be coming face to face with circumstances beyond our control.

After arriving at Euston Station, we were transported by a single-decker bus to Uxbridge, an RAF camp for boy entrants; clerks and accountants etc. There were about eight other men on the bus, which meant 12 of us were travelling in the same direction and for the same reason. Our stay at Uxbridge was brief. We had a medical and were sworn in. I found the medical was somewhat embarrassing for it meant we all had to stand in a line, stripped naked and were each told to cough in turn while the doctor held our private parts. I had never seen grown men naked before and suddenly became aware I was no different to the next man. At the swearing in ceremony we stood with our right arms raised and repeating what was said by a senior NCO. Then we were rewarded with what was termed the "Kings Shilling". We were now Airmen.

Following the ceremony, we once again got seated in the bus and were transported to RAF Cardington in Bedfordshire. Cardington was famous for being the home of the airships R100 and R101. I still remembered the R100 when it flew over Birkenhead during our school holidays in 1930. The sight of the massive aircraft would always be remembered. Although the airships are now no more the hangars still stand and at the time were used for the training of Barrage Balloon operators.

It was near enough to 4 p.m. when we reached the end of our journey and were met by our Corporal who led us to our billet that was to be our living quarters for the next 6-7 weeks. I was allotted the bed nearest to the front entrance and on the right. Just inside the front door was the room occupied by the Corporal.

"Just take your time to become acclimatised to your new surroundings," said the Corporal. "I'll be back later to march you to the cookhouse." As I sat on the bed, looking at the scrupulously clean billet (and having no doubt who would be keeping it this clean in future) I heard remarks such as "God Almighty, even the hospital was hardly this clean." One of the Liverpool lads further down on the other side muttered. "I should've brought me mam; it would be right up her street." I looked up at the ceiling and said to myself, "God! What have I let myself in for?" It was then I added, "You're here now, so make the best of it and not moan. So be it!"

The crew we linked up with at Euston Station were mostly Londoners who had plenty to say for themselves so what with the remarks and chit-chat that passed to and fro, the atmosphere soon became more homely and matey-like. Even the lad from Liverpool in the next bed appeared more relaxed and he introduced himself. During the journey from Lime Street Station to London he had hardly said a word. He wasn't that much older than me but of the same build; a bit on the skinny side. He went by the name of Lewis.

We were soon informed that Thursday night was what was called "bull night'" when everyone had to get stuck in and have the billet up to scratch for the inspection next (Friday) morning. Not only did the floor and stove have to shine but the three biscuits (mattress) had to be set at the head of the bed and on top were the blankets and sheets folded in a distinct fashion. The bedside locker, or the locker on the wall above the bed, was also open for inspection. It was on that first Thursday night I came to realise how matey it was with everyone mucking in. It had the atmosphere of a close-knit family without parents.

It was after the first night meal of sausage and mash followed by apple pie and custard; we were introduced to the NAAFI [1] It was something of a relief to find somewhere we could meet for a beer and purchase all our needs.

On Saturday morning we had to parade in one of the massive hangars, where we had to sign forms and be given our service number. Mine was 627762. Like our Co-op number 33901 it was easy to memorise. From there we were marched to the clothing store for the issue of our uniform. It was not unlike the 50-shilling tailors in Grange Road. One fellow with a tape measure had me standing with legs apart and arms outstretched and calling out the sizes to the other one on the other side of the counter. Before I knew it, I was standing in the line with an armful of clothing. Besides the jacket and trousers plus underwear I was then given my cap (which had to be changed about three times) and then the heavyweight top coat.

Sunday was free but we were left to polish the buttons and cap badge plus a canvas type waist belt of air force blue of which had to be "Blanco'd" to make it white. Anything up to three treatments was required in order to get it presentable. To be quite honest we felt it a waste of time for we hardly wore it after completing our 'square bashing', as it was called.

That is how we looked on the Monday morning. We were no longer individuals, we were now known as 'A' Flight.

A Flight - RAF Cardington 1938 (Photo: Sutherland Family Collection)
{That's me, at the back on the extreme right.}

On our first day on the parade square we were blessed with bright sunshine. Our instructor was a Sergeant who first put the corporal through the drill manoeuvres as an example to us. Our first lesson was how to march, something I took for granted having been taught in the scouts. I soon came to realise not all were blessed with this obvious skill for no sooner were we on the move, then first one and then another was forced to change step. From where the Sergeant stood, it must have appeared a right shamble. Constant drilling for the next four days had us march like a team. It was not only quick march but also slow march and the art of a reverse turn. Sounds like a dancing lesson but I can assure you there was no waltzing about.

We got to the point of proving our training wasn't in vain. Having marched around the square umpteen times we received the order. "*Squad Halt.*" and to our surprise every man came to a halt, bringing down the right foot which sounded as one. It was like music to the ears, and brought a smile to the face of the Sergeant.

It was on the Friday we were issued with a rifle. So once again we were entertained by the Corporal demonstrating the new routines. It usually began with "stand at ease" with legs slightly apart and the butt of the rifle coming to rest on the ground, the right arm outstretched with the hand holding onto the weapon with a firm grip. On the command "attention", the right arm and rifle would once more be in line with the body and the feet placed together. When told to "*shoulder arms*" one would lift the rifle to waist height and grab the butt with the left hand, pull it across the body and let it come to rest on the left shoulder. To "*present arms*", the rifle would be brought down with the left hand and moved across the body to meet the right hand and held in line with the chest and nose. The trigger would be facing outward. Once again it was a case of practice and patience.

We were feeling weary with the constant exercise but also felt proud at having reached the point where we moved like a team and were also receiving compliments on our performance from the Sergeant. Rifle drill continued on the Monday and Tuesday, then on Wednesday morning we went to the rifle range. Once again it proved how incompetent we were as not one of us hit the target. I feel our problem was that we were all unprepared for the repercussion when squeezing the trigger. In the afternoon we played a game of footy, like schoolboys with the kick and run type of game.

On Thursday morning we were directed to a room with chairs laid out in an orderly fashion. We were in for a lecture on venereal disease. I was on the learning end and amazed at the information received. I was the youngest of our group and at a loss when certain remarks caused smiles or even laughter. At the second lesson a week later, I was more prepared, having been lectured by the older airmen in the hut, especially by those from the London area who were only too keen to offer their knowledge of life in the "Big Smoke" as they called it. Their description of the different type of prostitute was hilarious, making the subject a big joke. I looked upon it as free entertainment, as well as education.

Having become settled, time seemed to go that much quicker and I was surprised when the Corporal informed us we were being granted leave for Christmas starting on Friday 23rd December.

On the Thursday we had a full-dress parade with the C.O. and Adjutant standing on a dais and marching to the Station Band. What a difference it made marching to a band, it seemed to make it that much easier. Having returned the salute, the C.O. and Adjutant made their way to the officers' mess and so be it, the parade was dismissed. We had the afternoon free in order to prepare for our departing on leave the following morning.

The next morning, we had to parade in front of the billet and be inspected by the Sergeant before boarding the bus to Bedford Station. Our manner of dress included the top coat and gloves plus our small kit carrier. The carrier was a small canvas type bag of air force grey and used for the likes of our shaving kit, soap and flannel plus brush and comb and Brylcreem. It was attached to a long strap which was passed over the head and came to rest on the shoulder. It was an early breakfast that morning so we were ready and waiting for the transport.

Whoever arranged our journey was spot on for we only had a short time to wait before boarding the train to Leicester where we changed for another train to Crewe via Birmingham. When I arrived at Crewe I had time to go over to the other platform and catch the train to Birkenhead via Chester. Alighting at Rock Ferry Station it was then a ten to fifteen minutes' walk to reach home. The front door was answered by my younger sister who cried out "Cor! Look what the cat's dragged in." On entering the living room, I was stuck for words, not knowing what sort of a reception to expect. For a brief moment not a word was spoken then Pop cried out. "I can't believe my eyes! You've not only put on weight, but grown a couple of inches." It was good to see the beaming smiles from both Mum and Dad. Such a reception enabled me to relax. "By the looks of you," said Mam, "you've been fed well. I agree with your dad, you look fantastic." I later realised I had only been away for a month, so such a transformation must have come as a shock to them, especially as they had doubts about my enlisting. Being Christmas, it was time to visit or be visited, but whatever it was an excuse for Mum and Dad to show me off. When shopping down at the market on the Saturday one would think I was the only one from Birkenhead in the RAF and come to think of it I probably was. Not only were heads turned but the comments made were most complimentary. "Now you have given them something to talk about," chuckled Pop. "You are something of a celebrity." Although quietly pleased with the attention created I also felt somewhat embarrassed.

During the week when enjoying a lie-in Mum entered the room and while trying to look busy questioned as to what was known as "loose women". I was pleased to put her mind at rest when informing her of the education classes plus the added information from the older men in the billet. Christmas dinner was something special and at tea time we had the usual sherry flavoured trifle.

Having to return to camp on the Friday was to some degree, a sad moment, but now fully aware of my situation Mum and Dad were both able to send me off with a smile. We had only one more week of square bashing in order to complete our basic training, and life became more bearable. On the Monday the Corporal came into the billet wanting to know if anyone wished to take part in the boxing tournament on the Wednesday and Thursday. As to be expected nobody was that keen to take part. The Corporal tried to put pressure on me into putting my name down. "You won't get hurt," he said dolefully "any sign of being out-boxed we stop the fight." "A bit late then," I replied. It was then to our surprise Lewis, one who wouldn't normally say boo to a goose, put his name forward. As it turned out he won the tournament with ease and we ended up celebrating in the NAAFI. Following a couple of beers, he let the cat out of the bag. He was a member of the Nel Tarleton boxing club in Liverpool. Nel Tarleton won the Lonsdale Belt outright in 1934. He also told us how, as part of his training, he was lectured not to go looking for a fight. Come Saturday morning we had our passing-out parade, once again marching to the Station Band and ordered to turn our heads to the left as a matter of respect for the Station Commanding Officer, who returned the salute.

It was on Monday 9th January 1939, and now burdened with our kit-bag, we were transported by bus to Henlow, not far from Luton. It was here we were to spend six weeks basic trade training in preparation to our becoming Flight Mechanics. The move was very much a matter of jumping out of the frying pan into the fire. On arrival we were introduced to our living quarters which was a hangar with rows of double-tiered bunks. We were surprised to find some of our new "room-mates" were sailors, training for the Fleet Air Arm. Our cosy atmosphere now gone it was a case of accepting the situation and making the best of it. As it turned out, our neighbours in navy blue were most friendly and they also did what they could to create an atmosphere that brought us closer together. During the daytime we were confined to the workshop, tackling a "test piece". The test piece was something of a trial, being a piece of metal one inch thick and about 6" x 4" in size. In the centre a hole had been drilled and it was now up to us to turn the hole from being round and made into a square. We seemed to be doing nothing else but cutting with a hacksaw or getting to the right size by way of a file. I can assure you it wasn't done in a day, more like a week. Having made the square hole to 1" x 1" we then had the job of converting a piece of metal about 5" long and 2" square so that one end would fit firmly in the hole. Just as well we weren't pushed for time.

Every now and again the Sergeant would make an appearance and indicated he was quite pleased. Then, having encouraged you to stick at it, would move on. Following a healthy evening meal, one felt more relaxed and prepared to lie down on the bunk and listen to the chit-chat. That is until one of the sailor boys encouraged us to have a small gamble on a card game. I don't remember what it was called. He had us place a bet on any card. If the card was turned face up before the Joker was found we won. Our penny (the stake) was turned into two pence. An alternate bet was on the four corners at four to one or a line at six to one. I might add, this game proved most popular. Another game we also played was the dice game of "Crown and Anchor".

Now allowed out of camp in the evening, I decided to book out and venture into town. It turned out to be a bit on the small side with the larger shops being on the left-hand side. Now closed for the day the atmosphere was somewhat on the dismal side. However, one shop stood out for the large window was fully illuminated and the products (mostly furniture) were well laid out. The window dresser deserved full marks. Directly opposite was a radio repair shop where I became attracted to what appeared to be a 12" x 12" inch box with a glass screen reflecting the interior of the Savoy Hotel in London, with Vic Oliver [2] putting on an act with Carroll Gibbons [3] and his dance band in the background (Vic Oliver was married to Sarah Churchill, daughter of Winston Churchill). I found out the following day I had been watching what was called a television set, an invention of which was expected to become popular although very expensive.

Our six weeks stay at Henlow wasn't all that exciting so I was pleased when we were posted to St Athan in South Wales. It was there we spent the next 6-7 months training as Flight Mechanics. It appears we were the first squad to arrive at St Athan, it having just been established as No4 School of Technical Training. [4] On that day 17th March, we paraded in the hangar and formed two lines. The introduction procedure ran at a snail's pace and allowed us time to gaze around. While studying those in the line opposite I caught sight of an airman I felt I knew. He was also staring at me the same way. When the parade was over he approached me and said "I know you don't I, you are Don Sutherland." "Yes," I replied, now aware I was right, "you are Kenneth Williams." It so happened, Ken and I sat at the same desk for the three years we spent at Temple Road School. That meant we had not seen each other since July 1935, a matter of four and a half years. He was accompanied by his cousin who lived on the estate at the back of our house on Dacre Hill. Small world isn't it? Although in separate classes we still met and chatted about old times. Usually at meal time or on a Sunday after Church Parade .

To give you some idea of the crew I was now billeted with. I am the respectable looking one, once again on the extreme right.

Outside our Billet at St Athan Mid-1939 Don is on the right.

(Photo: Sutherland Family Collection)

They might seem a "right-looking outfit" (and so they were), the course had an atmosphere of mirth, but also companionship. There again, at something like a Church Parade you would not recognise them as being the same crew; they were well drilled. As you will note, we were allowed to wear civvies on the Sunday so took full advantage.

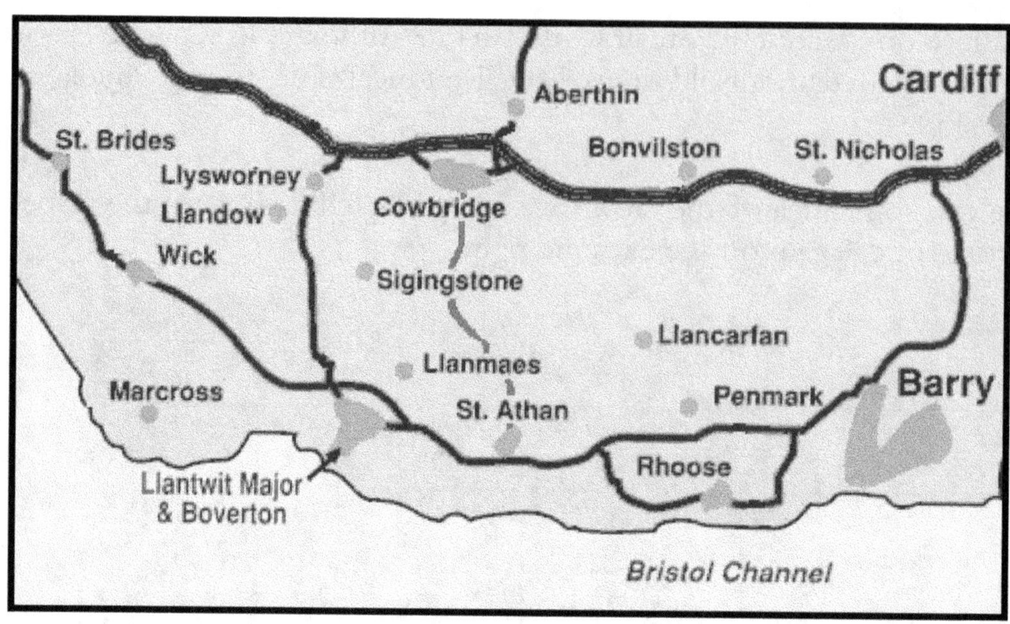

Here is a map giving you some idea as to where we were situated, showing the most popular places we tended to visit.

Cowbridge is a picturesque market town about 5 miles from camp so if one had the privilege of a camp bike it wasn't all that far away. On the other hand, if you were taken to there by motor transport and missed the last bus at 9 p.m. it wasn't that far to walk back. From memory, for all that Cowbridge was just a small town they had about five pubs. So, what with the Welsh beer and Welsh locals a sing-a-long was most appreciated.

Just prior to our arrival the railway had established a station at St Athan solely for our benefit. We were now linked up to Cardiff, Barry Island, Llantwit Major and Bridgend. Very convenient! Although the smaller of the group, Llantwit Major was quite attractive and the folk were very friendly. They too had some of our favourite pubs, The Old White Hart and the White Lion.

Barry Island was also popular (being a holiday resort) so we did not go short of a fish and chip meal.

Now having taken you on a brief tour of the area, I will return to everyday life at the camp. Our posting to St Athan, in order to continue our training, turned out to be a major change in life-style. A lot of pressure had been lifted because were now accepted into the RAF and not just rookies any more. We were now technical trainees; future tradesmen of importance, with a certain respect for our position. Unfortunately, we were still lumbered with billet inspection but nowhere as severe as at previous stations.

As mentioned earlier, we were also allowed to wear civvies on the Sunday except in the event of a Church Parade. We were also expected to show our respect by saluting any officers.

During my six to seven months at the camp in South Wales, a number of incidents happened that I particularly remember:

No1 - When blessed with a camp bike and off to Cowbridge with a mate from our billet it was one of those nights when it went dark early so we had to rely on the bike lamp to lead the way. About a mile out from camp I was attacked by bats . I saw the odd one in the rays of the bike lamp but not the ones that hit me on the head and chest. My mate thought my outburst was funny because he had been attacked before. "They won't hurt yer," he cried out, "they are attracted to your bike lamp."

No 2 - Talking of blows to the body and head, it was at that time we met Tommy Farr, British Heavyweight boxing champion, who had just returned from the USA having gone the full distance with Joe Louis, the World Champion. Such an exhibition of guts and determination had him top of the list by all Sports writers. Tommy was born in Clydach Vale near Tonypandy up the Rhondda Valley, only a bike ride from St Athan, so was able to take advantage of our gymnasium in order to train for his next fight. He was getting prepared when we arrived for our physical session and although we did not shake hands, we were formally introduced. Having watched him perform against two other boxers I had no intention of taking it up as a sport. He was getting in shape to fight Larry Gains at the Cardiff Football Ground on 22nd May 1939. He won the fight in the 5th round when Gains retired with an injury to his hand.

No3 - The Saturday when about five of us took off to explore Cardiff, the Welsh capital . We had in mind to catch the last bus back at 9 p.m. but we just missed it. "Left a minute ago" said a local. "It was almost empty," he added, "so decided not to hang about." For the next few minutes or so, we stood in a group munching fish and chips. "Now what do we do?" said one as he threw his greasy paper into the bin. "We'll just have to hitch-hike," came a voice from the back. "It's no good standing here and praying to the fairy godmother." "I agree," said another wiping his greasy chops, "but does anyone have any idea how far it is back to camp?" The know-all then decided to add to the misery. "From memory, it is about 20 miles. 15 from here to Cowbridge then 5 to camp."

"God!" someone cried out, "we'll be lucky to get back for breakfast." Having got directions from the bystander we walked to the main road leading to Cowbridge and began to thumb a lift. As luck would have it, it was only a matter of minutes before a man pulled into the curb and questioned our destination. "Back to the camp," we replied in a chorus. "Climb aboard," he said without a second thought. Minutes later we were getting comfortable and thanking our lucky stars. Unfortunately, our luck was short lived for about 5 miles out the driver pulled into the curb and cried "Here we are then, right outside the camp." It turned out to be the RAF Barrage Balloon maintenance depot in Llandaff, some 5 miles out of Cardiff. "But we are going to St Athan," one of our party muttered. "I am sorry", said our good Samaritan, "but this is as far as I can take you."

"Now I know where we are," said Mr know-all "it now means it is only 10 miles to Cowbridge, plus the 5 miles to camp." "Only," someone muttered, "it now means we will be back to square-bashing and back to marching at quick time." "Just think how lucky you are," someone added with smirk, "you don't have a rifle to carry!" This response proved we still had a sense of humour.

Apparently, we were getting close to Cowbridge when someone asked the time. Following a pause, someone answered, "About one o'clock". "God almighty!" the questioner muttered, "I should be in bed by now." A Scouser cried out, "Does yer mam know yer's out?"

To relieve the drag from Cowbridge to the camp, we had to rely on singing songs, such as *It's a Long Way to Tipperary* etc, plus relating the odd funny experience to each other. Every so often, when some form of seating was available, we stopped for a smoke. We finally crawled into camp about 6.45 a.m. and were met with an eerie silence. It was now a case of sneaking into our billet, hoping not to wake anyone, shed our boots and socks and stretch out onto the bed.

As luck would have it, Church Parade had been cancelled so were able to sleep until midday and then following a quick wash and brush-up, made our way to the cook house and we were blessed with a typical Sunday roast followed by trifle.

Such an experience was not forgotten in a hurry and from then on, I was quite happy with a night out in Cowbridge with a pint of ale lasting all night. I mentioned the sing-along earlier and how the Welsh locals, with their vibrant voices did not require any form of encouragement. It so happened, we were also blessed with the Howell brothers from the Rhondda Valley who were billeted next door. It wasn't long before someone would call out "Taffy, give us a song." The response was their rendering of *Danny Boy*. They were fantastic.

During March, April and May of 1939, I appeared to be on a roll regarding positive personal experiences but this suddenly came to a halt on June 1st when we were informed the Submarine HMS Thetis had sunk during sea trials with 99 men on board having perished. It was known that many of those killed had been dockyard workers. Thanks to the organisation of our Station C.O. all of us from Merseyside were soon to be transported by bus from the camp to Birkenhead. [5]

It was something of a morbid journey for us as we had relatives who were linked to the submarine during the time of its construction. My father had worked on the Thetis from the time the keel was laid and had been aboard when it went through underwater trials in the basin. The sub was launched in June 1938 and it wasn't unusual for me to go aboard and have a cuppa with Dad. We were not allowed to make tea in the joiners' shop.

It appears a torpedo tube had been left open and when opening the inner door, the water rushed in causing the sub to go down nose-first.

Having travelled all night, it was about 10 a.m. when I arrived home and to the surprise of our mam. It was then I had to explain the reason. "Not to worry," she said in a low voice, "your dad is upstairs in bed; he has quinsy, an abscess in his throat. He has been sick for the past ten days and put it down to the time when the sub failed to surface in the basin. Dad reckons it was freezing down there." I waited until lunch time before going upstairs and sighed with relief when I saw him safely wrapped up in the blankets. Unfortunately, he could not speak but the look on his face showed delight at seeing me again.

I stayed the night and returned to camp on the Saturday. From all accounts, we had all returned smiling. In the weeks to follow the tragedy was front page news with first one party and then another being accused of not making any attempt to rescue the trapped men.

Back at St Athan our life became more serious with our schooling taking on an all-new attitude. Our tutors were determined to have us complete the course with honours. Once in our billet after the evening meal it was a case of revision on the lecture of the day. Like me, the odd one was confused on certain points of technical tuition (we were in the practical period of our training now, not written) so we had to rely on our more learned room-mates to explain the issues in a language we understood. We benefited greatly by viewing an aircraft engine that had been dissected to show the inner parts, the feeling of uncertainty being somewhat dissolved.

On July 26th I turned 18 years of age, but not having the nerve to broadcast the event, it came and went. During the early part of August, we sat our written exam, followed by an interview with an inspector who tested our knowledge from a practical point of view. We all passed with flying colours.

We had to wait for our formal ending of the course and our "graduation", the outcome of all our sweat and tears. A stint down at the gym or kicking the ball about helped alleviate boredom. In the weeks to follow, the news mostly related to Neville Chamberlain (Prime Minister) who was doing everything in his power to avoid war with Germany. I was reminded how my parents had warned me about impending war when suggesting I change my mind about enlisting. It became obvious to me they knew what they had been talking about.

It was on Friday 1st September when Germany invaded Poland, and on Sunday 3rd September, England declared war on Germany. In the cabinet re-shuffle to follow, Winston Churchill became the first Lord of the Admiralty.

The thought on all our minds was "Where do we go from here?"

✝ ✝ ✝ ✝ ✝ ✝ ✝ ✝ ✝ ✝ ✝

DESTINATION UNKNOWN (SEPT 1939 - DEC 1939)

World War II was declared on Sunday 3rd September 1939.

It turned out to be something of a coincidence for only a week earlier we had completed our training as Flight Mechanics. The fact we were now classified tradesmen meant nothing on that mournful Sunday for we spent all day filling sand-bags. Added to the gloom of such a chore was the news the guard on the main entrance was to be doubled. At least we had someone to chat with. Although armed with a rifle awaiting the arrival of any Germans, we were told to keep a watch on members of the IRA. It was suspected the Irish Republican Army was about to take advantage of the situation. In the weeks to follow, small groups were posted to RAF stations throughout the U.K., except for one large contingent posted to Singapore. Among those was Ken Williams who sat alongside me for 3 years when at Temple Road School.

My posting came on Friday 15th September and accompanied by Charlie Pitcher (a well-built Canadian) and Harry Stowe, a true Londoner, I travelled to Gosport in Hampshire. We had never heard of the place. We arrived there the same day and were escorted to our billet in a large two-storey building. I was directed to a spare bed on the ground floor whereas the other two went upstairs. For a short time, I felt like a little boy lost but was soon put at ease by first one and then another airman who helped to unload my kit-bag and store my clothes in the locker above the bed. The blanket and sheets were already folded the same way as prior billets so I was soon able to stretch out and endeavour to relax.

On the Saturday morning we had to report to the sick-bay for the usual check-up and I was somewhat surprised to have a female doctor scan my bare body. "You'll pass," she muttered and noted my leaving her surgery in haste. Charlie Pitcher felt the same way for as I mentioned, he was well built. Harry Stowe lapped it up for he fancied himself with women. He was soon to earn the nickname of Popeye for quite often he would return from the shower naked and endeavour to flex his muscles. Not having his false teeth in made the image even more like the cartoon character.

Following the medical we had to report to the orderly room of our new outfit AACU. [6] It stood for Anti-aircraft Co-operation Unit. The office was in one of the hangars with the C.O.'s office leading off the main area. Having handed over our documents to the Corporal in charge, we made our way back to the billet just at the right time for lunch. Grabbing my mug and irons (knife, fork and spoon) I was soon in the queue for my sausage and mash, followed by crushed apple and custard.

Come Monday morning it was a case of attending the parade conducted by the station C.O. and accompanied by the station band. We were then inspected by our sergeant who would soon to let you know if you required a haircut.

Blackburn Shark. Designed as a torpedo bomber and spotter aircraft to be carried on aircraft carriers the Shark was a contemporary of the famous Fairey Swordfish "Stringbag" and in many ways was a more advanced design having a fully metal fuselage (the Swordfish's fuselage was fabric covered). The later marks of Shark had an enclosed cockpit while the Stringbag had an open cockpit. The performance of the two aircraft were virtually identical. Nevertheless, it was the Stringbag that was kept in production because it was easier and cheaper to build. The Shark was relegated to second-line duties like target towing. (Photo: Editor's Collection).

Once the parade was dismissed our unit then marched to our hangar (No1) where we then went about our duties. The hangar door now open, planes were pushed out onto the tarmac (the large area between the hangar and control tower). I was finally approached by an airman who introduced himself as Corporal Harris who told me to follow him. We didn't go far before we stood alongside a Shark 1029 [7] bi-plane, an older type aircraft with a radial engine. "Here she is, Don," he said with a wry smile, "This is the aircraft you are expected to maintain. So, the best of luck." For a moment I stood there gawping, not knowing what to say. For all I had been trained as a Flight Mechanic everything we were taught was by way of theory.

Obviously aware of my thoughts he placed his hand on my shoulder and endeavoured to console me. "Not to worry," he said in a low voice, "I will show you how it works and if you become uncertain at any time, ask me or another mechanic." Somewhat relieved, I was soon sitting in the cockpit, starting the engine and scanning the important instruments.

Having thanked him for his assistance and patience he returned to the hangar. At that moment in time I suddenly realised I was now in another world and yet unaware as to what was to follow. During the course of the brief tuition I was to learn the Shark 1029 had been fitted with a long contraption to house a large target, plus the winch by which to operate it when target towing.

It was while endeavouring to look busy I caught sight of a building situated behind No's 1 and 2 hangars and was later informed the Gosport RAF Station was referred to as Fort Rowner. I could now see why. [8]

Fort Rowner

In the early stages we had to do guard in the fort, which was dark and dingy and had a musty smell. It was a relief to do your stint out in the open and inhale fresh air. Guard duty became commonplace at that time and if not in the fort it was around the hangars.

On my first guard duty around the hangars I was accompanied by a Corporal Hailey, a member of the NDC (National Defence Companies) [9] who were there to guard the base and billeted in the next billet to ours. During the drab duty of guarding the hangar, I suggested we stop for a smoke but became aware he was one of the old soldier types and did everything by the book, so I let him march on and joined him when he came back.

It was during that period we were kept busy with flying time, Shark 1029 in particular, for it was the duty of AACU to co-operate with the Naval Gunnery School operating at the Marine barracks in Eastney. It was during this time I had my first flight in the old Shark, standing in the rear cockpit with Trevor Verrior, an LAC wireless operator who was there to operate the winch and so manipulate the target. I wasn't of much help but enjoyed the view and came to realise why a W/Op was required to govern such an operation. Having gone back and forward a few times, Trevor sent a message to those at the school by way of an Aldis lamp and read the message returned in the same fashion (there was no other way of communication.) My next flight was "solo", passenger-wise that is! Sergeant Willcox was the pilot and it was an "air-test" flight of the aircraft following a forty-hour inspection.

In the weeks to follow there was nothing all that exciting to break the monotony. We waited at the same time each morning and afternoon for the arrival of the NAAFI wagon. A cup of coffee and a rock cake was most welcome. If lucky enough to purchase a warm and fresh rock one was always tempted to buy another one, but if they had been baked a day earlier they were definitely rock cakes. Another cake, we referred to as a "door-stop" was a fruit slice and believe me it could be used as a door-stop! But there again it was very filling. The following weeks became something of a tedium; it was a case of plod on and try to look busy. On the odd day weather conditions grounding all aircraft it was a case of sitting in the crew room having a natter and the odd smoke. The situation relating to those poor sods in France was uppermost in our minds so obviously became the main topic of our conversation.

With Christmas fast approaching, arrangements were being made for Christmas leave and as to be expected; all those living in the lower half of England went on leave on Friday 22nd December while we northerners had to hold the fort until their return. Come Christmas day the parade had been cancelled so we ambled over to the hangar and debated what to do in the meantime. "All right you men," said the sergeant rigger in his usual calm voice, "we have a request from the Naval Gunnery School who wish for us to arrange a target-towing exercise for the benefit of Winston Churchill who is about to arrive there any time now." "I suppose that means 1029 is required?" I muttered. "We have no option" was his reply, "as they want a target and not a sleeve."

"The fact Churchill is there to see how the trainees are coping," said LAC Dobson. "What say we paint *Merry Christmas*, on the target?" The response was unanimous, so within minutes they had the target spread out on the floor and two riggers armed with paint and brush got stuck in. The paint used was known as dope and it dried in a matter of minutes.

With the sergeant now satisfied, the target was rolled up and placed in the compartment along the side of the Shark, which was then pushed out onto the tarmac. With the chocks in place I climbed aboard and started the engine. With the usual two men spread over the tail of the plane I opened the throttle and checked the instrument panel for any defects. It wasn't long before Sergeant Willcox and Trevor Verrier were aboard and once the chocks had been removed they moved out onto the runway. The time then was about 10.30 a.m. and near enough to 11 a.m. the crowd had dispersed, leaving Jack Knowles (rigger) and myself to await the return of 1029. It was at that moment in time, whilst leaning against the door frame of the hangar having a smoke, I saw the snowflakes falling. Although not heavy in numbers they were extra-large. "Christ almighty," I cried out "that's all we want." "They should be on their way home," said Jack, shaking his head from side to side, "so will need to fly low to find their bearings."

As we spoke, the snow appeared to becoming heavy and what is more, it was showing signs of forming a blanket. With a sigh of relief, we heard the sound of the engine and seconds later saw them emerge from the screen of snow and make a perfect landing. Sergeant Willcox then taxied up to the hangar and with the aid of a tail-wheel trolley we soon had the machine put to bed. Speaking to Trevor,

Jack asked "How did it go?" Trevor replied, "No way were they trainees, the target took a pasting." By the time we returned to the billet and
prepared for our Christmas dinner, the snow was inches deep and following the traditional chicken dinner plus bottles of beer, the snow was at least six inches deep and still coming down. Armed with a couple of bottles of beer I returned to the billet and prepared to settle down and relax. There were three more bods there at the time but within the half hour they were gone. I soon became aware I was the only one in the block, upstairs and down. I lacked any entertainment owing to the fact the wireless had been returned to the shop it was hired from. I managed to find some reading material left on the table so for the rest of the day drifted into another world. Although a load of rubbish it was at least readable. Following the evening meal of cold chicken and chips followed by trifle I returned to the billet, kicked off my snow-covered boots and pulled my bed out to get the benefit of the wood burner (fire), poured out a beer and stretched out once more with my book.

Blackburn Shark over Eastney ranges Christmas Eve 1939 (Painting JW Dell)

My bed was about the fourth one down on the right, so it was no problem pulling it out in front of the fire. It must have been about 7 p.m. when I stopped to pour another glass of beer and I realized how eerie was the atmosphere, for owing to that blanket of snow outside not a thing could be heard. It was near enough to 9.30 p.m. when I switched off the lights, bar one, and crawled into bed. That was the loneliest Christmas I ever experienced but on looking back, I just accepted the situation without any emotion. It was as just another day.

THE TIDE CHANGES (DEC 1939 - JUNE 1942)

On returning from my New Year leave in 1940, everything appeared to be functioning as normal; except of course for the effects of bad weather conditions when all flying would be cancelled, which created periods of boredom. When working in a group similar like AACU one can always expect a couple of bods finding something to moan about and subsequently becoming a pain in the backside. So be it. But one day they made their feelings known in no uncertain manner, but on this occasion a corporal from the orderly room was present and made his presence felt. He had the nick-name of Gannet owing to his always having something to talk about; he was a proper old woman. Such a description was rather unfair for besides being most helpful and cheerful the information he spouted was usually of interest, gained as it was from his position in the orderly room, the centre of our unit, housing the C.O. and Adjutant. "You might moan," he said, "but stop to think of those poor devils of the BEF in France. They are up to their necks in snow and standing with rifles at the ready." [10]

With a slight improvement in the weather, life slowly got back to normal with my plane (Shark 1029) busy target towing. Unfortunately, it was mid-February when I came face to face with another disaster, this time relating to the plane I looked upon as a pet. It was mid-morning when they took off in weather quite reasonable, but when half way through their operation fog came in from the Solent and caught them unawares. It was a real pea-souper with Sergeant Wilcox soon to lose his bearings. He turned north hoping to find a church spire or the Guildhall clock; anything to give him some idea of his position. As mentioned earlier they were without any means of communication (no radio contact) so were left to fly on looking for a break in the fog and maybe find somewhere to land. Unfortunately, they reached a point when a lack of fuel forced them to bail out. It appears they were somewhere over Birmingham. Trevor landed in front of a house and came face to face with a woman brandishing a carving knife. When bailing out he pulled his flying helmet off and found he was as deaf as a doorpost on landing. He was unable to hear what the woman was screaming about and was rescued by a passer-by who recognised his blue shirt and black tie which was now exposed with his flying suit having opened during the bail out. It was later that afternoon when Gannet came from the orderly room to give us the news. It appeared both were in good shape but they had yet to find the whereabouts of 1029.[11] The bad weather conditions hung around for the next 2-3 days, so still no flying. Once back to normal I was assigned to a Blackburn Skua, a much more modern craft which were being used on our aircraft carriers.

The Blackburn Skua was designed to be both a fighter and dive-bomber. Like the Shark it was meant to be operated from aircraft carriers by the Fleet Air Arm. Skuas had a short and intense combat career in the Norwegian campaign in early 1940 and in the Mediterranean the following year. They were extensively used for second-line duties such as target-towing. (Photo: Editor's Collection).

Having been broken in on 1029 it did not take long to become accustomed to the Skua. The Skua was fitted with a Bristol Perseus X11 Radial engine plus a Coffman 6 Barrel Shotgun Starter. When climbing aboard each morning and starting the engine it was a matter of turning a switch which in turn sent a current from the battery to the Coffman starter which ignited a cartridge that exploded and set the engine in motion. When it came to opening up the throttle in order to check the instruments and listen for the sound of something not quite right, it was necessary to have tail support. Invariably two each side of the rudder would suffice.

Holding the tail of a Skua down during engine run-up. (Photo: Editor's Collection).

The instrument panel looks confusing but I was only responsible for the ones relating to the engine performance.

It wasn't long before I had my first flight in the Skua and that had to do with a number of foreign pilots having been posted to our unit in order to become familiarised with our aircraft and gain flying hours. On this occasion the pilot was a Pole detailed to do a flight test. I was looking forward to seeing the view from the Skua. It was my job to sit in the rear cockpit armed with a note book, a pencil and clock. Having reached the first point, he informed me we were at 10 thousand feet and about to turn to point two. The information, plus the time, I recorded in the book. I then sat back for further instructions at point two which read now 11 thousand feet turning to point three. I recorded the information until we reached 13 thousand feet. I was so frozen that I found it almost impossible to hold the pen and clock. Unlike the pilot I wore just a thin flying suit over my overalls. When we landed, someone relieved me of the book, pencil and clock while another airman helped out. So much for the view I failed to see!

Blackburn Sharks in the foreground with Blackburn Skuas flying overhead. This photo was taken at Lee-on-Solent, only a few miles from Gosport. Note the cockpit canopies on the Sharks, a refinement over the open cockpits of the more famous Fairey Swordfish. (Photo: Editor's Collection).

Now into April and with much improved weather, I was offered a flight with Nobby Clarke (our dare devil pilot) [12] which included low level and high dive-bombing over the Naval Gunnery School at Eastney. On each low dive-bombing run he would increase his height until at about 10-12 thousand feet he would keel over and go down nose-first like a stone. On such an exercise I would be standing up in the rear cockpit with a chain linking my parachute harness to the floor. So be it! When in the dive my body was almost horizontal so it was a case of hold on mate and hope for the best! On each occasion we would reach the height when I thought it was time he should pull out for the Gunnery School, but Nobby had to give them value for their money! He would leave it for a few seconds more before he pulled the stick back and changed our direction from nose down to horizontal. It was at that point I felt my stomach was somewhere down between my knees. Moments later I could see the time on the Guildhall clock, what a relief! On more than one occasion Nobby would invite naval or army officers and give them the flight of their life. Unfortunately, it was I who had to clean up after them!

It was about that time I ribbed a room-mate by the name of John England as to his being all done up like a dog's dinner (Liverpool expression). He had changed into his dress uniform and was wearing shoes. John, a reserved type of individual but most friendly explained how he was off to Southsea for a dance in a church hall. "You can come with me if you like" he said with a reassuring smile. "I can't go like this," I replied. "Get changed and look respectable," he suggested while shrugging his shoulders, "you've got plenty of time" I couldn't believe I was being invited out, it hadn't happened before, except of course when going out with the gang at St Athan. "Can you dance?" he questioned. "Yes," I replied, "but it has been quite some time since doing a soft-shoe shuffle" (once again a Liverpool expression). A short time later we were catching a bus for the Gosport Ferry, boarded the ferry to Portsmouth, and caught another bus to Southsea. It wasn't far from the bus stop when we entered a large hall at the rear of Saint Judes Church.

No sooner were we in there when my escort disappeared upstairs to the canteen which was run by women who made tea and coffee and a range of sandwiches. Most of the seats were occupied by females so I was undecided where to park my bum. Not knowing a soul, I felt a little embarrassed. It was then I heard a voice call out, "Do you want a seat?" It was then, almost alongside of me, I noticed two girls moving over to make a space for me. With a sense of relief, I thanked them and sat down. They introduced themselves as Rita and Thelma, so I returned the compliment by introducing myself as Don. Within minutes I was amazed how forthcoming they were with all three of us conversing in an adult fashion. Not like some girls who tended to make a remark and burst into giggles.

Of the two, I was most impressed with Rita who was most attractive and immaculately dressed. Unlike most of the girls who were dressed in a skirt and blouse or frock, Rita wore a most expensive looking two-piece outfit with a blouse and to top it off she spoke without any sign of an accent. She reminded me of the Queen making her speech on Christmas Day. Unfortunately, a friendship with Rita did not start straight away. My rigger Jack Knowles, who had also joined the club, had become besotted with a girl named Muriel who had a friend called Beryl. He asked me to make a foursome. Without thinking I agreed. Beryl wasn't in the same street as Rita, but she was at least a fantastic dancer. I had no feeling of romance with Beryl so our acquaintance was quite formal. At that time the thought of "getting a girl" evaded me. I not only lacked confidence but realised one could not take a girl out without a certain expense being entailed. It was then, as if it was meant to be, I got 14 days confined to camp and so was an absentee at the club. During that short spell, the situation changed. Beryl had cottoned onto another mechanic from our unit, so I was reprieved. Rita was tied up with one of our riggers (Harry Beaby) who lived in Portsmouth, which meant I was now going "freelance".

One evening when having the last dance, I saw Rita standing alone and looking bewildered so I guided my partner over to her and asked what was wrong. It appeared Harry had taken off without as much as a goodbye and left her stranded. "Stay there," I almost ordered, "I will be with you when this dance has ended." Inwardly I felt mad at such behaviour so was only too pleased to be walking her home, wheeling the bike. It was just around the corner from Goodwood Road when I decided to say good night and endeavoured to catch a bus down to the harbour. I don't know why, but I gave her a kiss goodnight and for a moment felt embarrassed, but soon felt at ease when noting how she had accepted such an act. "Will I see you tomorrow?" she asked, in her polite voice. "I'm not sure," I muttered, "I could be on guard." "What about the next night?" she questioned. It was then I had to open up and explain my financial situation. "That is no problem," she murmured "here is two shillings." From that point on I knew she was the girl for me and held her in high esteem. The following night I could not get over to Goodwood Road quick enough. For two so young we acted like adults, having respect for each other. Having arrived unexpectedly I found her having just washed her hair but she insisted we go for a walk. In the conversation to follow, it appeared we had a similar upbringing. She went on to explain how although she was head girl of her school she was unable to extend her tuition at the higher school for, according to her mam, she could not afford it. So be it, she left school at fourteen and went out to work. The one thing that gave me some pleasure that night was the fact I appeared to have been accepted by her mother and young brother Danny. I also discovered that Corporal Hailey of the NDC, who I had shared guard duties with, was Rita's father!

My lifestyle seemed to change overnight. From that point on, time seemed to fly and before you know it we were into May. From the news we learnt the German army had invaded France so our boys were now preparing to hold them back. Other than that, information was curtailed somewhat, so it was a case of plodding on as per usual. With my Skua now fitted with a winch it had extra flying hours in order to tow a drogue over the Gunnery School. The loss of the Shark had proved a disaster for the trainee gunners for they lacked the practice of firing at a full target. With ships now open to air attacks it was essential the gun crew were up to the task. Such being the extent of extra flying hours, my Skua had quickly reached the point of a major overhaul. So, working in conjunction with a skilled fitter, I was faced with stripping the engine down to the last nut and bolt. While at the same time Jack Knowles and another rigger went about their duties regarding the airframe. Also involved was an instrument fitter, Eddie Binns. He was a quiet type but enjoyed a bit of fun. Using a hoist, we were able to pull the engine away from the bulkhead and lower onto a bench.

For the next couple of days, I seemed to be doing nothing else but wash parts in a bucket of petrol. The pistons had been removed to allow inspection of the sleeves. We then had the job of reassembling the engine, which entailed fitting new rings to the pistons. Following hours of work and a lot of patience, we had it ready to be put in place. It was the following morning when we were on the last lap of assembly we were paid a visit by our commanding officer accompanied by an officer of higher rank. Following a quiet conversation, the senior officer turned to us and said "I want this aircraft ready to fly by 4 p.m. today." Having accepted our salute, he left the hangar and disappeared. Following a short lunch break we eventually had it towed out onto the tarmac, not far from the hangar. It was then 3 p.m. Not having time to perform an air-test it was my job to climb aboard and start the engine, just idling at first and every so often give it full throttle. As time went on, Trevor Verrior made several trips to the plane and placed cartons in the rear cockpit. Eventually, both he and Sergeant Willcox arrived in full flying gear and climbed aboard. As ordered it took off at 4 p.m. Aware such a flight was unusual no one had a clue where it was going.

Having knocked off that much earlier I took off for Southsea and when alighting from the bus at the pier, I saw a number of soldiers running like mad to awaiting transport, most had trousers rolled up to their knees and their boots slung around their necks. Such a scene was unbelievable. Making my way to Osbourne Road to the cafe where Rita worked (a bit of a nobby outfit), I stood outside watching her cleaning up. When aware of my presence I was invited inside by her boss, Mrs

Forer, and was served with a plate of beans on toast. It was fantastic!

On the way home, I described the scene at the pier. Rita said she had heard of an ex-neighbour, who had a boat, being told to assemble at a certain point and to await further orders. We wondered what could be going on but finally gave up thinking about it. It was two days later when my Skua returned home accompanied by Nobby Clarke [13]; and Bill Phelan in the other Skua, when we were informed of the situation on the other side of the English Channel. "God!!" cried Trevor, shaking his head from side to side, "you should've seen it. It was a complete shamble with hundreds of army wallahs being rescued from the beach at Dunkirk." It appears they had been towing flares in order to put light on the situation. Skuas from another outfit were shot down.

The evacuation of British forces started from May 26th and went on until June 3rd.

It was but a fortnight later Rita reached the age of 16 and it was to be a month later when I turned 19. As I mentioned earlier, we were but a couple of teenagers playing the part of grown-ups and making a good job of it. I put it down to acting with a sense of maturity and personal respect.

On June 4th Churchill made one of his famous speeches. "We shall fight them on the beaches." It was now obvious we had our back to the wall and there was nowhere to run and hide. According to a speech by our Station CO on parade the following morning, it was fully expected we would be invaded any day from now on. Such an assessment of the situation was quite understandable for the Germans had invaded and defeated all the countries in Europe with ease and now had their sights on us. As Churchill said, "The battle of France has come to an end, so now the Battle of Britain begins." Such was the sense of panic; the CO had ordered a large trench to be dug at one end of the drome. It was at least 12ft long and 4ft wide by 5ft deep. I happened to be one of the numbers detailed to stand in that trench all night, armed with a .303 rifle and 5 rounds of ammo. We had been ordered to keep an eye open for German paratroopers and aim to kill. As luck would have it the weather was quite mild but, as to be expected, it was pitch black. First one would light a cigarette then another, informing those above we were waiting for them. The arrangement was such a shamble, first one fell asleep then another. Come dawn's early light we came to realise we had been attacked but hadn't fired a shot; the enemy turned out to be mosquitoes. The worst casualty was Harry Stowe who had both eyes closed and swollen to the size of golf balls. Thankfully the exercise wasn't repeated the next night but guard duties became more regular.

About a month went by without any sign of attacks from the air. It was then in July 1940 the Germans made their presence felt by attacks on shipping, ports, radar stations, airfields and factories. The 10th July was looked upon as the starting point in relation to the "Battle of Britain". The so-called "black-out" had been in force since September 1939 and was now rigorously enforced. The atmosphere was somewhat weird without any sort of illumination, be it from street lamps or car headlights. At least it gave one confidence to stroll hand in hand, especially the shy ones!

With circumstances so unsettled and at times under pressure to return to camp on time, I was introduced to a way out across a large grassy area at the rear of the billet. It was here railings had been installed dividing the camp from a right-of-way leading down to the main road. I found a gap in the iron railings just big enough for me to squeeze through. So be it! I started to not bother to book out at the guard room. Going out was no problem owing to it being pitch black, but returning the following morning meant scanning the area before squeezing through the railings and making haste to the rear of the billet. Once inside it was a case of a quick change into working gear and then off to the cookhouse for breakfast. My sleeping arrangements at Goodwood Road were either the settee or two chairs.

Come August, the Luftwaffe appeared to penetrate our defences with little or no problem and concentrated on airfields and radar stations. It had become obvious Hitler was intent on breaking down our air defence before making his final move. So-called "dog fights" between British and German fighter planes had become common, with such a battle taking place thousands of feet high in the sky and making it almost impossible to distinguish the Spitfire from the German Messerschmitt. Every so often, one would see a plane going down in a spin, followed later by a pilot floating earthward in his parachute.

On Friday 16th August, having just sat down to breakfast, the senior corporal from our orderly room took the seat opposite. "You are late for breakfast," he said with a wry smile, "I've just seen you coming in the back way and as you know, I could put you on a charge for such an offence." I had to agree, but was somewhat surprised coming from such a decent man. I had yet to see him report anyone regardless of the offence.
"It so happens," he continued, "you can do me a favour." "What's that?" I questioned. "we have received a signal from someone high in rank who wants us to arrange volunteers for a job to be executed in the Isle of Wight. I haven't a clue as to what the job entails so am in the dark as much as those who volunteer." "It

appears you have me by the short and curlies," I replied with a grin, "so that being the case you can put my name down." "Thanks Don," he murmured with a sigh of relief. "You can forget parade and return to your billet. Get your small-kit organized and report to the armoury at 10 a.m." On his way out he gave me a pat on the shoulder.

Promptly at 10 a.m. I was outside the armoury but was told to await the arrival of the armoury officer. A short time later, two of my mates arrived accompanied by Yorky who was a machine gunner on station defence. One was Peter Mock who was a boy entrant, due respect for his higher degree of knowledge [14]. The other was Jock Allen who was one of the quiet types, but still most sociable. Both were flight mechanics from AACU. As to be expected, Peter questioned our presence but following a shrug of the shoulders we assumed it was to dig graves for German aircrew; a task we had performed before. Nearby stood two airmen who, by their dress and manner gave away that they were typical rookies. They had probably just finished their square bashing. Knowing how they must have felt, we approached them and once aware they were in the same boat as us it was introductions all round. Almost right away they relaxed and entered into conversation. It was some time later when the armament officer arrived in a flat tray truck; the sides being no more than 18 inches high. "Right you men," he cried out, "load these picks and shovels onto the truck and then your small kit." (a small bag containing shaving gear, soap and toothbrush, etc). Seeing the tools reinforced our expectation to be digging graves. The officer disappeared into the armoury then eventually emerged with two Corporal armourers. Jock glanced at his watch and muttered, "Gord! Look at the time - no wonder I'm hungry, it's bloody near one o'clock." It was at that moment that sirens sounded and not only did we hear the drone of aircraft when Peter cried out "Oh my god!! Look at that lot." while at the same time pointing into the direction of the officers mess. One did not require binoculars to see what he was getting at, for there were at least a dozen Junkers 87's approaching. It was then we heard the command, "Get down into the shelter, quick!!" It was given by a Sergeant from TDU (Torpedo Development Unit). [15] Nobody had to be told twice and we moved like rabbits down into a burrow.

Within minutes, the ground shook and dust could be seen filtering down from the roof of the shelter. Opposite sat two WAAF's trying to comfort each other, both as white as a sheet. All I could do was light a cigarette. It was soon obvious we were in for a pasting like other airfields, and wondering how long it was going to last. It was then as if out of the blue we heard a couple of Hurricanes fly over and someone cry out "Here come the cavalry." Sighs of relief could be heard throughout the shelter. Not until the all-clear had sounded were we allowed to crawl back into the open and left to gawk at the damage inflicted. One hangar was almost flattened and our hangar next door was badly knocked about. Outside the hangars, planes having been parked were now upside down. We looked upon the scene with amazement. Our view of the devastation was short lived for we were ordered to climb aboard the truck and get the hell out of there.

Ju 87 "Stuka" dive bomber of the type that raided Gosport. Although relatively slow they delivered their bomb-load with great precision. (Postcard: Editor's Collection).

With eight of us, plus the picks and spades, it was some minutes before we were sorted out. As the officer in charge was about to board the comfort of the passenger seat, he suggested we keep our eyes open in case they came back again. Shaking our heads from side to side we mumbled," We will be like sitting ducks."

For all the truck was something out of the ark, it wasn't long before we passed through Fareham and on the road to Southampton. Once again, we were trying to guess our final destination and never thought for one moment it would be Calshot. Calshot was an RAF base not far from Southampton used by flying boats and float-planes.

Having been escorted to our billet, we wasted no time finding the cook-house and a long overdue meal. We were subjected to another air raid that night but no damage was reported. Come 8 a.m. the following morning, Saturday 17th August, we were sitting down to a hearty breakfast. By 10 a.m. we had loaded our gear (including picks and spades) on to an RAF motor boat and transported to Ryde,

Isle of Wight, which was known for its long pier and soft sand.

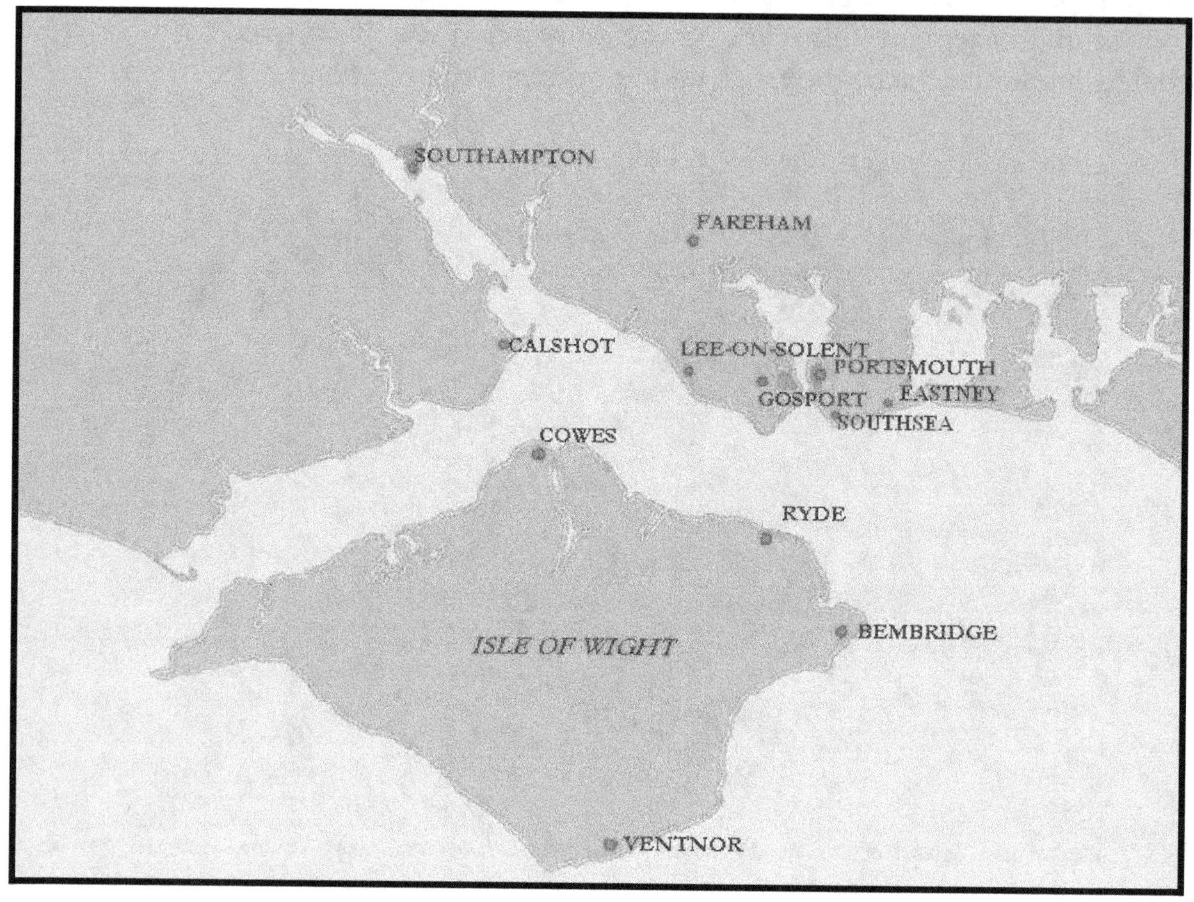

Map of the Solent area showing locations mentioned in the text. You can see the huge detour the party took from Gosport to Ventnor via Calshot. You would have thought that a better and much quicker way to get them to Ventnor would have been for the RAF marine craft to have picked them up directly from Gosport harbour or one of the float-plane slipways at nearby Lee-on-Solent.

Having been dumped on the beautiful beach it was a case of sitting back in the sun, watching kids makes sand castles and young people sunbathing. While waiting for the train to Ventnor due in at approximately 2 p.m. we had ample time to relax while eating a cut lunch.

We had boarded the train for Ventnor which I remember had wooden slat seats but was nevertheless quite comfortable. We arrived at Ventnor about 3.30 p.m. We were greeted by a middle-aged man who was there to transport us to our digs with his flat-tray truck, similar to the one that carted us to Calshot but minus the sides and tail-board. With this type of vehicle, we were able to sit with our legs dangling over the side. The digs turned out to be quite comfy with ample room. Jock and I were directed to the front bedroom on the left, with the bay window.

Postcard of the Clarendon boarding house. (Sutherland Family Collection)

The landlady was most charming as was her 16-year-old daughter who was there to assist with the running of the establishment. Following a most tasty evening meal, with a second helping of afters, Jock and I decided to venture down town to find a suitable pub. It so happened we were in Grove Road, so found it most convenient to walk down the hill to an old but most attractive pub called *The Crab and Lobster.*

Inside had a quaint atmosphere. It was quiet, with only the table nearest the bar surrounded by patrons enjoying a relaxing pint of ale. Having entered the dim-lit surroundings we purchased our half pint of mild and selected the table to the left of the entrance and sat down. Our conversation was nonchalant and relaxed, or rather we attempted to be, because we were still in the dark as to why we were on the Isle of Wight. Then the old fellow seated at the next table leaned across and asked if we had arrived to dig out the unexploded bombs. "What bombs?" cried Jock. "Those up on the hill at the RAF station," he replied. Being at a loss to offer any explanation, we just shrugged our shoulders and muttered "Yeah! You could be right."

Minutes later, we had a pint of beer placed before us, plus best wishes from the old fellow and those at the other table close by. On the way back to our digs, we were stuck for words. When we got back to our digs, with the rest of the gang now in bed, or close to it, we kept the information about the unexploded bombs to ourselves.

The information did not stop us getting a good night's sleep, and following a most appetizing breakfast it was all aboard the old truck and the slow ascent of the hill up to the peak of Boniface Down, the highest point on the Isle of Wight. Some 10 minutes later we arrived at the target of our mission, a scene dominated by large pylons. The Radar station of Ventnor. [16]

Ventnor "Chain-home" Radar station, Isle of Wight. The tall masts on the right were the transmitter masts, the smaller ones on the left were the receivers. High up on the hill behind Ventnor they gave excellent coverage out over the English Channel. (Photo: via Paul Tummel)

It was then we were informed as to reason for our presence. The area in line with and beneath the pylons contained 5 unexploded bombs awaiting our attention. [17] "Before we proceed," announced the officer in charge, "it will be necessary to fill sand bags and protect the building nearby, plus what appears to be a transformer." Nothing was mentioned as to our safety and it was only minutes later the officer bade us good day and left us to the job!

After his departure, we looked inside the building nearby, now deserted of personnel. It was the operations room, where the job of detecting approaching enemy aircraft was done. Amongst the discarded items inside I found a pair of brown shoes, just my size! An item that attracted our curiosity was a safe, which we man-handled outside. For light relief, on breaks from work, we set ourselves the task of opening the safe. The lock proved a fiendish puzzle to overcome. It was some three days later that somebody succeeded in finding the code. The contents were only a coil of copper wire! On that first day our search of the building didn't last that long before one of the corporals suggested we get stuck in and fill the sandbags. Once again, our task wasn't easy. We had to move quite far away from the site in order to locate an area where we could find soil loose enough to handle for filling up the sand-bags.

As luck would have it, the weather was reasonably good with a clear sky. Later in the day we observed another terrific air raid flying over to hit Ford, Lee-on-Solent and our own base of Gosport. God knows how many enemy aircraft were involved for they appeared in droves and appeared to evade any weapons of defence. We had been warned by a red signal [18] so automatically searched the skies. Jock and I plus one of the new bods who tagged on walked around the main building and were blessed with a panoramic view across the English Channel and its approaches to the mainland of Hampshire. It was from that point we saw the German bombers make their approach toward the mainland of Hampshire. [19]

The time of that raid was about 2 p.m. so we spent the final three hours sandbagging. Following dinner, we just smoked or prattled on about anything or nothing. The only mention of the bombs was when Peter mentioned our lack of appropriate gear; such as sheer legs and extraction tools. The Corporal armourer agreed and added "We'll just have to manage one way or another." We didn't need any rocking to sleep that night, for the physical effort of sandbagging had tired us all out. The following morning it was back aboard the truck and we were on our way back up the hill.

We stood in a circle around bomb number one, waiting for someone to come up with a bright suggestion. The bombs had only penetrated the ground by about fifty percent and stood about waist high. We soon saw why, for when striking the pick-axe around the bomb we had sparks flying from making contact with flint-like boulders. It was a case of seeking a gap between the shiny rocks and aiming at it with the pick. Having penetrated the crack, it was a case of levering the tool to ease out bits of rock, and once removed by another person we would then aim for a similar spot. The pace was slow and a lot of patience was required. First one person would have a go then pass the pick over to another. There were only room and tools for two men to be active at one time, and the rest stood around as spectators. Having "broken the ice", so to speak, we made progress and got the bomb uncovered until it was now chest high. It was at that point someone noticed what looked like one of the fuses so it was suggested by one of the armourers that we have a go at removing it. We had a problem in not having an extracting tool so we had no option but to attack it with a copper drift [20] and a hammer. First one had a go and then another but to no avail. "Something's wrong here," said Peter, "it should come out easier than that." Nobody appeared to have an answer. Then following a pause, Peter cried out, "Stop hammering anti-clockwise and try going in the opposite direction." Sure enough, he was proved right for it showed signs of moving and soon it was far enough out to extract it by hand. [21] It turned out to be shaped like a piece of rock; Blackpool rock, but not red or sweet. It was a solid piece of sulphur wrapped in paper with German writing on it and measured about 6" long and near to 2" wide.

Feeling a bit more at ease we dug down further in order to get at the other fuse. Now having the knowledge of how to go about it, extracting the other fuse was easy. By this time the bomb was damn near shoulder high but still stayed firm in the now large hole. Standing back pleased with our effort, we were joined by the officer. "You have done well," he cried, "You deserve a lunch at the cyclists' cafe."

The cafe was popular with those touring the Isle of Wight by bike. "Before we go," said the corporal "do you think we could have the truck pull the bomb out of the hole and lay it on its side?" "I don't see why not," the officer replied. So, without further ado we had a rope securely wrapped around the bomb and hitched to the truck. The operation proved to be easy and we soon had the bomb lying on its side on the outer side of the hole. Having coiled the rope, we climbed aboard the truck for our downhill trip to the cafe. We were about half way down the hill when, surprise, surprise saw the bomb blow its top! We looked in awe at the fountain of stones and dirt. Even to the point of Orr!! Lunch turned out to be something special - bacon and eggs and fried bread.
By 2 p.m. we were back at work on bomb No 2 making quick progress now used to working the flint-like rock. What amazed me was the attitude adopted following the explosion of bomb No1 and having observed the damage it caused. On the odd occasion we would stop to listen for a ticking sound, it was obvious we were all aware of what the outcome would be if it went off but we put on a brave front. It was as if one wasn't allowed to look scared, so there was a circle of forced smiles and droll remarks.

We worked through the afternoon, but still had a way to go. We paused our digging and took a break to enjoy the excellent view point (being nearly 800 feet above sea level). We then saw enemy aircraft approaching from our left, it was so low we were looking down on it. It was about to enter the Channel and make for home. At the point when it was in line with us, the rear gunner turned to fire in our direction He had obviously caught sight of the white vest of the new lad which made it easy for him to set his sights. The sound of gunfire was not very loud but when we saw the tracer bullets coming towards us we fell flat, face down. We were blessed with dense fern about chest high which thankfully gave us some coverage. A few seconds later we took the chance of being safe and got to our feet. It was at that moment two RAF fighters arrived from nowhere and shot it down. It was still floating on the water when Jock cried out. "Awhar noo – we've had our entertainment for today." We all lacked any real knowledge of German aircraft, but we felt certain it was a Heinkel 111 bomber. [22] So we went back to work.

Soon we were collected by the truck and once more called it a day. During dinner, it was announced that the matron in the children's home across the road was to celebrate her birthday the following day and we were all invited. So, the next day we managed to reach the point of removing the fuses and were quite prepared to leave it as it was. Following the lunch, that awaited us on return to our "digs", it was a matter of having a wash and endeavouring to appear respectable. However, Jock and I decided to give it a miss and stood at the window of our room, looking down at the asthmatic kids having fun and games with our lot and the nurses. The playground was up to the right side of the main building.

The "Children's Home" Don remembers is now St Catherine's School, Ventnor.

Having the advantage of a bay window our attention was caught by the sight of a plane that seemed to appear from nowhere. At first, we thought it was a Blenheim but soon realised it was a German plane when we saw bombs falling from it. The scene down below in the play area was briefly one of panic, but was soon under control by the quick-thinking nurses and our men.

Out of curiosity, Jock and I made our way over the hill and down to the scene of destruction. The houses were mostly three storeys high so we were amazed to see one house with the front missing, as if cut with a large knife. It was like looking into a doll's house from the back. Up on the bedroom floor stood the wardrobe only a matter of inches from the edge of the floor, or what was left of it. Even the bed was close to the edge and still looking respectable. What a sight! Both Jock and I were approached for advice but suggested they speak to the Air Raid Wardens who thankfully, had arrived on the scene. Amazingly the conversation that evening did not dwell on the subject.

On Wednesday morning it was straight onto bomb No3, having left bomb No2 as is. Surface conditions did not help any owing to concentrated flint-like rocks. Once again it was a case of cocking an ear for the sound of ticking, the warning sound of bomb activity. Although finishing a bit earlier, it was decided to let bomb No4 stay where it was until the morrow and we sat back and enjoyed a quiet relaxing smoke.

Thursday was the same, with bomb No4 keeping us busy until about 4.30 p.m. with bomb No5 still untouched. It was while awaiting our evening meal, we were told a message had arrived indicating we were to return to Gosport the next morning. The news was received with a sigh of relief.

At approximately 9 a.m. on the Friday morning while waiting for the bus to Ryde, we heard an almighty explosion from up on Boniface Down. "Sounds like our mission is complete," cried some bright spark. The remark was accepted by all, while at the same time we realised what the outcome would have been had we been back to work as normal. Minutes later the bus arrived and we were on our way, minus picks and shovels.

The ferry trip from Ryde to Portsmouth was most relaxing, followed by the voyage to Gosport. Another ten-minute trip on the bus had us walking up the road past the married quarters into camp and to our respective billet. On entering our quarters, Peter and I were greeted by Taffy Evans who, for some unknown reason was sitting on his bed looking somewhat mournful. No sooner had we passed the time of day than the siren went, indicating an air raid warning. Without hesitation Taffy got under his bed for cover. Peter and I looked at him in dismay but decided to carry on as normal by unpacking our small kit and placing the items in their respective places. Later when preparing for tea we soon noticed not all our room-mates had returned from work and the atmosphere was rather doleful.

Not until reporting for work the following morning did we come to realise the reason for such a gloomy atmosphere, for it was then we saw the damage created by the air raid we had witnessed on the Sunday from Boniface Down. Besides material damage we were informed that quite a number had been wounded and seven had been killed. From what we could gather, the seven killed were the fire crew. The lack of numbers related to those who had gone home on unauthorised leave. [23]

A short time later we, the so-called bomb disposal squad, were detailed to dig out the bombs around the petrol dump. The task turned out to be much easier than at

Ventnor for not only were the bombs much smaller, they had been sabotaged by the factory workers. [24] It was our job to scramble down the hole and place the bomb in a bucket which was then hoisted up to the awaiting armourers who removed the fuses. It was then they became aware the contents were sand and explosive. Owing to the two drastic bombardments changes had been made. All serviceable aircraft were now parked across the drome at what was termed the dispersal, a strip of land sheltered by a wooded area. A crew room had been erected containing a desk and a wood burner type fire; the latter becoming most welcome as winter approached. Come September the so-called Battle of Britain came to an end owing to the fact daylight had become shorter and the Luftwaffe were now concentrating on night bombing. Our lifestyle became somewhat unnerving when forced to gather in the air aid shelter, sitting in the dark and listening to the drone of German aircraft in the cloudy sky above. Above the racket of ack-ack gunfire one became accustomed to the sound of a bomb on its way earthward and following moments of deathly silence, the sound of the explosion when they landed not too far away. Every shelter seemed to have its "experts" who would speculate on where each bomb had dropped.

Each night I wasted no time in making my way over the harbour to Southsea to spend the night in the shelter with Rita, her brother Danny and her mother. Unfortunately, each night the skies above Portsmouth became full of enemy aircraft not only targeting Portsmouth itself but also heading for the likes of Southampton or Bristol. In the event of an enemy aircraft being damaged by gun fire they could well drop their load over Portsmouth while making for home. I still used the gap in the railings to get back into camp each morning while at the same time living in hope all transport was functioning as normal to get me back on time. I did get caught out on one occasion but had sufficient time to make a detour and cross the harbour on the car ferry.

The military situation that autumn not only increased flying hours over the gunnery school but also increased guard duties. It so happened that Rita's father was the Corporal in Charge of the guard on more than one occasion and billeted in the next block to ours. Being a member of the National Defence Corps, he was confined to camp and welcomed my report each morning to tell him the family was safe.

For all that October was unnerving November was somewhat terrifying, with the Luftwaffe showing no mercy for besides London being target number one, other cities received a pounding, including Coventry on November 14th. The raid was carried out by 515 bombers from Luftlotte 3 and in that one night 4,000 homes were destroyed with about 600 people killed and 1,000 injured. From all reports,

50 parachute bombs had been dropped and 36,000 incendiary bombs. The parachute bomb was very destructive because it did not penetrate the ground on landing but exploded at ground level, meaning the blast spread over a wider distance. These bombs often killed people in air raid shelters by sucking the breath from their lungs; they died from suffocation. Such bombs could flatten a whole street.

Prior to Christmas, Jack Knowles (my rigger) and I had become a foursome with Rita and his girlfriend Muriel who lived in Goldsmith Avenue. On the odd occasion we treated ourselves to a show at theatres such as the Theatre Royal and were entertained by Billy Cotton and his band, or Geraldo. [25] On most nights it was a case of picking up Muriel at her home then venture out to the club at St Judes.

Also prior to Christmas (in November), our unit was entered into a soccer competition and God knows how, but I ended up in charge of the selection of players and responsible for the gear. As luck would have it we were blessed with good players so found winning not too difficult. On the odd occasion Rita would arrive on the scene especially when we played on a Wednesday, and she enjoyed being a spectator. On more than one occasion when the game was over and returning to the billet she would be heralded by a chorus of wolf whistles and once indoors I would be got at by such remarks as "God! What does she see in you?" or "What have you got that I haven't?" Such jocular remarks were received in the same manner as intended, for one had to admit they were a great bunch of guys.

No 2 AACU Football team, Don on Front row on right. (Sutherland Family Collection)

The 5th Hants Volunteer Arms.

Thankfully we had some respite over Christmas 1940 and, unlike my previous Christmas which was spent alone in my billet with the outside deep in snow, I was invited to spend the day with Rita and her family. I gave her dad a special Christmas treat by taking him to the pub (the Volunteer Arms) He did not normally visit pubs so he was quite pleased to accept the invitation. The landlord was his neighbour.

Rita and Don (Photo: Sutherland Family Collection)

To add to the celebration, Rita and I became engaged. There was now no doubt as to our feelings toward each other. Our romance was not one of "wine and roses" but rather one blessed with a quiet acceptance.

On Friday 27th December, together with all those from "up north", I went on leave. The trip to Waterloo was relatively quiet until I came face to face with the hustle and bustle of London. I had to make my way to Euston Station via the underground. I saw those who had taken refuge down there from the air-raids. For all such a scene had a pathetic look about it, those concerned appeared happy enough and obviously appreciating the safety it provided.

It was only minutes later when I boarded the underground train for Euston and was soon rising up from the morbid depths on the escalator. Thankfully the train to Liverpool was soon on its way so I was quite happy to sit back and light a cigarette and become involved with the chit-chat in the carriage. On arrival at Crewe I managed to catch the train to Birkenhead via Chester. About an hour and a half later I was emerging from Rock Ferry Station and was faced with a ten-minute walk to my home on Dacre Hill. We lived over the Midland Bank as my parents were the caretakers. Although glad to see me the atmosphere was somewhat morbid owing to the constant bombing they had endured. By all reports Liverpool, Birkenhead and Wallasey had been subject to a right pounding. It was referred to as the "Christmas Blitz."

Everyone was expecting another raid, people were uptight and on edge. They openly indicated it could well be their turn that night to have their name added to the list of casualties. No matter where one went, the conversation was directed to the aftermath of such destruction.

I came to realise how we in the service were not informed as to all that was going on. London and Coventry had been mentioned but the likes of Merseyside, Southampton and Bristol were all but ignored. Had Liverpool been mentioned I would have been more concerned. I was surprised our mam failed to mention it in her letter.

To prove how close they became to the bombing, my sister Eileen described how she climbed out of the lounge window onto the roof of the Bank and assisted Dad to extinguish the number of incendiary bombs using a stirrup pump.

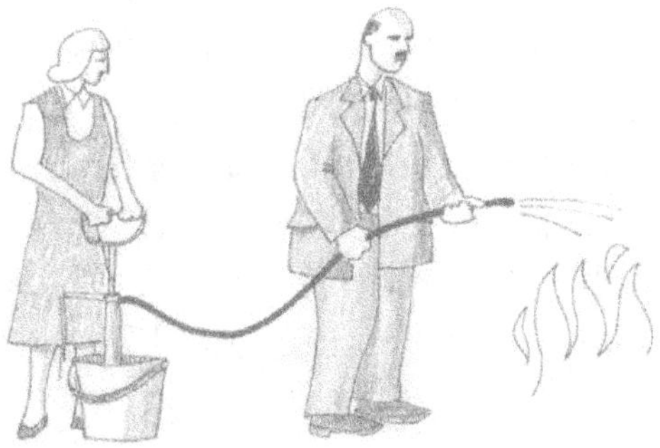

Using wartime stirrup pump.

You used the contraption by pushing the handle up and down like a bicycle pump which forced water through a spray nozzle at the end of the short length of hose. The stirrup pump became essential to all households for most air raids began with the dropping of incendiary bombs by "pathfinders". The fires started were used as a guide by the following aircraft.

As might be expected, New Year's Eve celebrations were somewhat quiet with most toasts relating to "peace and goodwill to all men". I wasn't all that sorry to return to Gosport on January 4th and once more get back into the fray of normal life.

On Friday 10th January when low cloud cancelled many flights we finished early. Having enjoyed an early tea, I was soon changed and ready for my usual trip to Southsea. While sneaking out through the railings the siren sounded. It was pitch black but no sound of activity so I walked down the right-of-way to the main road and just caught a bus to Gosport ferry. It was at that point the action began with sounds of gunfire and the drone of enemy aircraft. When alighting from the ferry on the Portsmouth side the captain made it clear he wasn't going any further. As was quite often the case I made my way to a pub nearby called *The Ship Anson*, and ordered my usual whiskey and dry ginger. The pub appeared quite normal with a number of dockyard workers from the nearby naval establishment being present. Taking time sipping on my expensive concoction I timed it just right on leaving, for moments later the trolley bus arrived, one of my options for reaching Albert Road, Southsea (the other option was the petrol driven bus). The trolley bus, being reliant on electricity, was handicapped by relying on overhead power lines. It was then the situation changed dramatically, for no sooner had I reached the top deck for a smoke, I saw a bomb explode in the naval barracks nearby. Seconds later I saw a number of sailors beating a hasty retreat from the barracks.

It was at that point the bus stopped under the overhead railway bridge, it being an ideal spot under the circumstances. Further down the bus about six passengers were on their knees with their heads under their seats. "We are not going any further" said the conductor, "so you can please yourself if you want to get off and walk." he added "We've already seen one bomb drop in the Guildhall Square and being wide open, we had no option but to keep moving. By good luck, this is an ideal spot for us to take shelter." The driver climbed down from his cab and joined us on the platform, lit a cigarette and mumbled "We are definitely the target tonight."

I paused a moment, but impatience won the day so I bid the crew farewell then broke into a trot up Park Road in the direction of Elm Grove. I hadn't got that far when I was joined by a couple of fleeing sailors obviously panic-stricken, having been so close to death by the bomb in the barracks. On the right-hand side of the road was a fairly high wall surrounding the barracks while on the left was the wide-open space of the United Services Cricket Club. It was the entrance to the ground that gave us a breather for the iron gate was surrounded by concrete pillars joined by a fancy concrete headpiece. It was only about 2 feet wide but gave us false confidence. Casting our eyes skyward we saw a Junkers 87 with its fixed undercarriage flying from the cover of one cloud to the next. The sight got us moving once more. Breaking into a trot I managed to reach the corner of Elm Grove and the High Street where I saw a faint light coming from the cellar of a large Georgian house so made for the steps and into the small room below. There was no sign of the owners but in the faint light of a 15-watt bulb I met a woman accompanied by her elderly mother. They also could not understand how the premises were vacant. "A bit rough out there," I muttered, to which they nodded by way of agreement

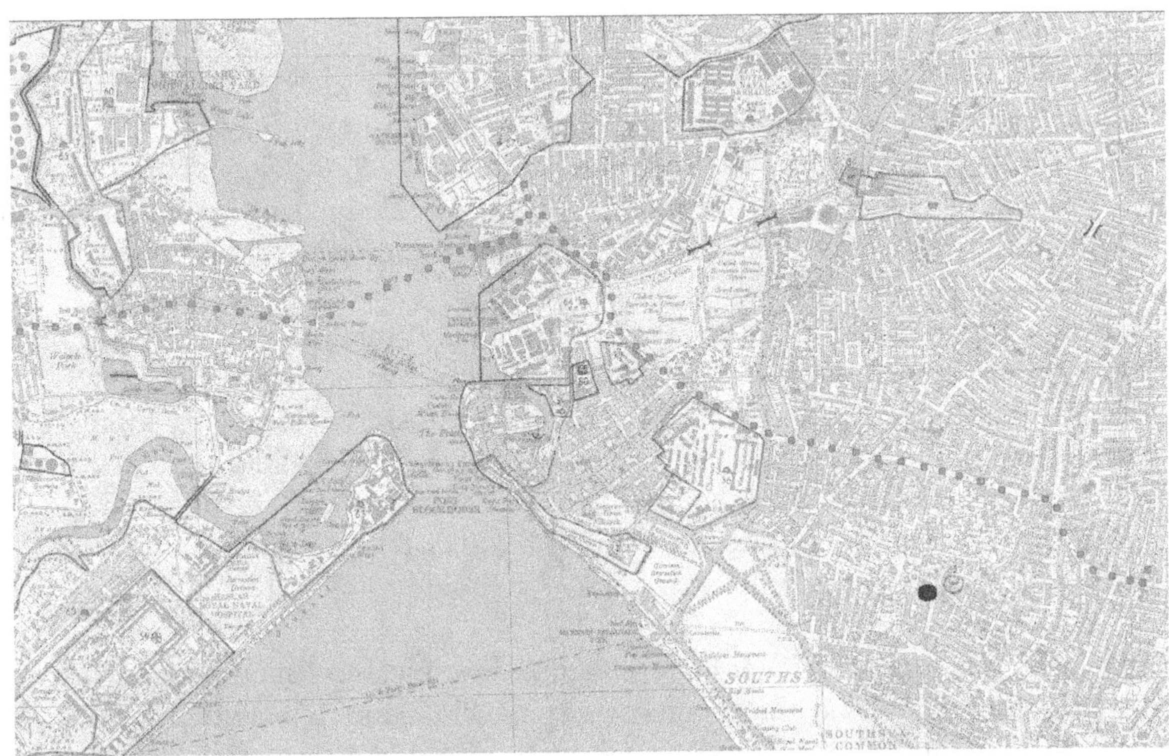

Don's route from Gosport to Southsea (red dots) on the night of the big "blitz" on Portsmouth superimposed on a German target map of Portsmouth. The large dot shows the location of the St Jude's club where Don first met Rita..

Trying to ease the tension I indicated the possibility of a lull which would enable them to move on. "I hope you are right," said the younger woman, "for we haven't far to go." Moments later and to my surprise, all went quiet. The guns on the common just down the road had ceased to fire indicating it was safe enough for the time being. "Now's your chance," I muttered. While they moved along the High Street I turned into Elm Grove. Now up to that point in time Elm Grove was looked upon as an elite shopping centre; anything from fashion garments to top class furniture, but the scene of destruction that greeted me had altered all that. I saw that not one shop had its windows intact. Each and every one was under the attention of the fire brigade. Spread out like a spider's web were the hoses from at least four fire engines and all were full of wee holes creating a display of mini fountains.

I turned into Albert Road, passing by the Kings Theatre, turning left into Goodwood Rd and into the shelter. My arrival came as a surprise. A quick movement of bodies allowed me space alongside Rita and her family. I gave them a brief report on my hazardous journey as well as giving them some insight as to the local situation we were faced with. "You took a chance," said Jack, the proprietor of the pub across the road. "but there again you were left wide open when leaving the bus."

Rita then explained how she and her workmate finished work early and were on their way home down Cavendish Road when a bomb dropped on the opposite side of the road. It did not explode as such but spewed out oil on the pavement and garden wall. [26] They made a bee-line for the nearest shelter only to find it locked up. At that moment an air-raid warden arrived and escorted them home.

The following morning, I had to take a short cut and catch the car ferry in order to cross the harbour to Gosport. When Rita arrived at work that morning she found it had also been bombed and Mrs Forer, her boss, was arranging to move the cafe to another shop across the road. She asked Rita if she had seen Thelma. When she said she hadn't she asked if she would jump on her bike to see if she was alright. Showing no sign of hesitation, she took off for Eastney but on her arrival found the street flattened; not a house standing.

By coincidence Jack, my rigger mate, suggested we pick up Rita and make our way to Goldsmith Avenue, the home of his girlfriend Muriel. Walking up the Avenue from Victoria Road everything appeared as normal, but upon entering the home of Muriel we were shown to the back door to see the view. What we saw was unbelievable for, as with Eastney, the whole of the next street was gone. The only building standing was the surface air raid shelter and from all accounts all those seeking shelter there were also killed. It was obvious it was the result of a landmine dropped by parachute and exploded on contact. Those in the shelter would have been affected by the blast from the bomb, which acted like a giant vacuum cleaner, sucking out all the air in their lungs, which meant they would have died instantly.

Having surveyed such utter destruction, we decided to make our way to the club via Victoria Road and we were pleased to note it was functioning as normal, if somewhat down in numbers present. Our first move was to climb the stairs up to the canteen and relish a coffee, a sandwich or a cake. One had to praise these ladies for the way they managed to cope every night of the week. One also had to praise the band of five musicians who also made their appearance every night. The first report to be released revealed 172 people had been killed with 430 injured. 47 were killed when an underground shelter at a school was hit. It appeared 300 German aircraft dropped 25,000 incendiaries as well as high explosives. 2314 fires were recorded and 60 water mains fractured.

For the next three months we were kept relatively busy because of increased flying hours plus extra guard duties. Also, during that period we had a number of overseas pilots arrive at our unit, mostly to become familiar with our aircraft or to keep up to date through flying hours. They would be our visitors for approximately 5 weeks and then posted to a more active squadron. I was surprised to be granted my annual leave on Tuesday 8th of April which meant I would be home for Easter. Having been informed a week earlier it gave Rita time to arrange some time off and travel up to Birkenhead with me. As it happened, the trip north was most eventful; a journey one would not forget in a hurry.

As with my previous trip for New Year the journey from Portsmouth Central to Waterloo was fairly quiet. Once in London we became embroiled in the activity of hundreds of passengers dashing from one station to another. On the underground railway Rita saw the number of people bedding down for the night (not only for safety but many probably had no home to go to). We bade them a silent good night at Euston Station and boarded the escalator going skyward to the main railway station. We had time to purchase a snack and a coffee at a NAAFI wagon parked nearby and located the platform leading to our train going north to Liverpool. We had luck in our favour and found an empty carriage and sat down on the outer side away from the corridor. Our privacy did not last long. Our compartment soon filled up with a mixture of naval bods and civilians, but also the corridor filled with army personnel lumbered with kit-bags.

For quite some time conversation was somewhat limited. The sound of train movement with its clickety-click acted like a lullaby. In the dimly lit carriage with its low blue light, the majority had dozed off. Such was the effect of the mechanical music even the army personnel in the corridor who were seated on their kitbags could be seen with their chin on their chests.

The one prominent civilian having studied his watch in the low light, mumbled "Won't be long before we are in Rugby, our first stop." It was at that moment Rita cried out, "Look at the sky over there, it appears to be on fire." The civvy was first to react, out of his seat and gazing out of the window, "It looks like Coventry is copping it again." he said in a posh accent. It was at that moment we noticed the train had slowed down, followed by the scream of an aircraft engine and the sound of bullets along the roof of the carriage. Instantly it was panic stations with everyone down on the floor in the hope of protection.

The next few minutes were interrupted by sounds of mumblings and mutterings. "Why the hell is it going so slow?" was one remark. "Such was also on my mind." said the civilian, "especially as there is a tunnel not far up the line." It appeared he was a regular traveller between Rugby and London and only too pleased to return home each night, if only for safety reasons. He was proved right for it was but a short time later we entered the tunnel and came to a halt. We all felt relieved and once more slouched down in our seats.

The length of the wait then began to create some impatience, with one mumbled voice suggesting the driver and fireman were making a can of tea. Eventually we began to move slowly, the sound of jolting buffers informing the guard all carriages were intact. It was on arrival at Rugby the posh civilian bade us good night. We were soon on our way to Crewe, a journey lasting approximately one hour.

We were feeling the effects of such a long journey while aware we still had a way to go. We changed trains at Crewe and caught the one for Chester and, so be it, the train for Birkenhead. That way we would steer clear of the trip from Liverpool. Unfortunately, our bright idea came unstuck for on reaching Chester we were informed we had missed the train to Birkenhead. Being near midnight, it meant our spending all night in the waiting room with no heating.

Obviously looking a bit worse for wear we were approached by a middle-aged man who enquired as to our dilemma and offered us a lift in his van. The van turned out to be on the small side and nearly full of newspapers. Thankful for small mercies, we clambered aboard and made ourselves comfortable by rearranging the bundles of daily papers. As to be expected, he had to make a number of stops at village stores and drop a bundle of his load on the doorstop now shrouded by a dark eerie silence. Eventually we reached our destination at the bottom of Rock Lane, which left us with a ten-minute walk to Dacre Hill. In response to my ringing of the bell it was some minutes before the door was opened by our dad. We were informed in no friendly manner by our mam it was gone two o'clock. Our brief explanation had little or no effect for she just shrugged her shoulders and said she was off to bed. Our dad, as usual, was more diplomatic and suggested we take a seat at the table while he made a cup of tea. While appreciating the cup of char plus a relaxing cigarette, we enlightened him on our eventful journey and explained the reason for our looking a bit scruffy. "Good God," he said with a heavy sigh, "you must be worn out. So finish your tea and get up to bed."

It so happened, sleeping arrangements were made that much easier by the absence of my youngest siblings, Fred and Doreen, who had been evacuated to somewhere in Wales while my brother Graham was now also away in the RAF. This meant Rita shared a bed with my sister Eileen while I had my bed up in the attic. As to be expected, Rita and I slept in until near enough 10 a.m. and were pleased to be greeted by Mum in a more amiable frame of mind. The reason being I surmised, Pop had spoken to her about her attitude hours earlier. "Come and sit down," said Mum in a friendlier manner, "breakfast won't be long." Fried egg on fried bread was most appreciated, not to mention a strong cup of tea. With Pop at work in the shipyard and Eileen in Lever Bros soap works based in Port Sunlight, the atmosphere was most relaxed.

Besides the hot cross bun on the Friday we had our usual painted egg on the Sunday. Taking advantage of the Easter holiday, I was able to introduce Rita to a number of family and friends who accepted her into the fold. All in all I was quite pleased with the friendly gestures and to be told she was one of the family. As to be expected, she was warned by way of the Liverpool humour as to what she could be letting herself in for.

Thankfully the return journey was not so eventful, probably because we were travelling during daylight hours. Once back to the unit it was nose down to the grindstone and no mucking about. The training of foreign pilots who were there for only a short period of time kept us busy and it was during such an exercise I came head to head with our Sergeant I/C over an engine fault. The fault in question related to the prop boss leaking oil. On the previous day it wasn't too bad but, on this morning, it had definitely become much worse. When opening up the throttle it poured out, even to the point of affecting the windscreen. Returning to the crew room I refused to sign the appropriate daily test sheet much to his annoyance, for he intended to fly the plane regardless. In the end we came to an understanding that he signs it first and I would sign afterwards. The transaction was witnessed by other ground-crew members. As scheduled it took off at 10.30 a.m. The two crew members were from Czechoslovakia. From what I could understand they were flying some distance and returning the next day. Come the middle of the afternoon we received notification of it having crash landed, but nobody was hurt. Aware that such a situation could have the flight mechanic arrested I immediately did my nana [27] in order to clear my name. I even went to the point of approaching the orderly room and putting in for a posting. "We can't do that," was the reply. "Under the circumstances I can only suggest you apply for another course. It will be more straightforward that way." So be it I ended up for a driver's course, which took about six weeks to materialise.

Don posing in front of Blackburn Roc L3085, an aircraft he helped maintain at 2 AACU Gosport. This adaption of the Skua mounted a Boulton-Paul turret with four machine guns behind the pilot. This particular aircraft was flown by "Nobby" Clarke and has his "saint" insignia on a yellow diamond on the fuselage. On 26th September 1940 the aircraft was involved with a fight with a German Heinkel He 59 twin-engined floatplane over the English Channel; an encounter described in detail by Nobby Clarke in his book "What Were They Like to Fly?". (Photo: Sutherland Family Collection)

BACK DOWN TO EARTH (JUNE 1942 - OCT 1943)

Mid-June 1942 I was informed I was to be posted to Weeton, North Blackpool. The news sounded exciting but it turned out to be something of a let-down for I saw very little of the famous holiday resort. Weeton was established some 12 months earlier specifically for the basic training of a number of trades. It was nothing to write home about, the living accommodation and the cookhouse turned out to be standard for the R.A.F. at the time. The classrooms were well laid out, giving the pupils more scope when preached to by the instructor. Subjects covered included dissected motor engines, giving some insight as to how they functioned. Carburettors were given similar treatment. The one part that lacked any attention was the gearbox and that spoke for itself (in loud tones) when we were introduced to the 30 cwt Crossley truck on our first couple of outings. The truck, dating back to about 1928, had what was called a crash gearbox and had to be controlled by what was termed the 1, 2, 3 manoeuvrings. When you pushed the clutch to the floor one had to count 1, 2, 3, select gear then repeating the process before allowing the clutch pedal to spring back. It was only then you could push the accelerator down and proceed forward. If the procedure was not adhered to you were notified by a loud scrunching sound, followed by foul language from the instructor. Once having mastered the gearbox we were promoted to the more amenable Austin car.

Crossley Truck.

Going back to the 1928 Crossley, I had sympathy for those living within a few miles, for when we ventured out in convoy in the dark of night to hear one learner endeavouring to change gear could be bearable, but when three to four passed one after another it would have had some poor individuals grinding their teeth. Not until the last two weeks of our six-week course did we venture into the big city; Blackpool. The main test was manoeuvring through the high density of traffic, including the tram. The tram caused problems for us trainees. Being linked to power lines, it was always toward the middle of the road and it was dangerous to overtake on the right-hand side. So be it, we had the problem of timing our way past on the inside when the last passenger had alighted or boarded the tram. It was then we put the foot down and shot past the slower vehicle.

Not until the day of my driving test, scrutinised by a keen inspector, did I come across another similar problem and that was linked to an RAF parade. Blackpool was the base for those posted overseas and although I had not been caught earlier by such a long parade it was now I came unstuck. On approaching the main drag and instructed to go straight ahead, I found myself having to stop at the junction owing to one of these parades. Under the impression one did not obstruct such a parade I stayed put and waited for the coast to clear before proceeding. The inspector had no hesitation to have me wait another week owing to "lack of confidence". He explained I should have taken advantage of the space created between the marching columns. So be it, the next week I spent viewing the sights of Blackpool.

On Friday July 18th I was posted to 172 Squadron in Chivenor, North Devon. Chivenor was approximately four miles from the proud market town of Barnstable. As to be expected, the journey from one end of the country to the other was not altogether exciting so I was thankful for the company of Harry Coles who was quite light-hearted and not at a loss for something to say. We had to change at Crewe, again at Birmingham and then Taunton, before being met at Barnstable. As it was summer, it was still light when we arrived so we were able to scrutinise our new form of accommodation, the Nissan Hut. We had heard of it before but they were not erected until new camps were established. [28]

Saturday morning was taken up with our visit to the sick bay for the usual incoming medical examination, followed by a tour of the essentials, such as the cookhouse and NAAFI. Our guide on this occasion was a Londoner by the name of Eddy Cayton. Eddy, slight of build, was a most amiable character and appeared young for his age. He was soon to become one of a trio for we hit it off so well, owing to the fact he was a fantastic pianist. A session in the NAAFI in the evening was most relaxing, with a beer in hand, and if he did not become vocal himself, he would sit back and mutter "Do you know this one?" to get you to sing along. Monday was the day of reckoning when we were introduced to our Sergeant Steadman (pronounced Stedman). He was well proportioned and gave one the impression he could eat you for breakfast, but I was soon to realise he was a real gentleman. His voice alone had a certain calming effect. One could sense a happy atmosphere when he introduced us to those drivers present, two males and two WAAF's, whose smiles and cheery responses made us feel accepted into a close-knit circle.

Chivenor MT drivers 1942. Don is on the middle row second from the right. (Sutherland Family Collection)

In due course we were allocated each a tractor which became our full responsibility. We were given a tour of the sites we would have to visit on our daily routine. No 1 was the petrol tank, which we had to visit in order to fill our petrol bowser. The bowser became an important part of our equipment in order to fulfil our daily chores, which included the filling of aircraft fuel tanks, (usually set in the wings). One had to tow the bowser and park in front of the wing, hand the nozzle of the hose to the mechanic on the wing and when certain he had it firmly in the opening we would start up the motor at the rear of the bowser and set the pump in action.

A fuel bowser in operation. (Photo: Pat French Collection).

Tractors were used for all kinds of tasks on RAF airfields. The most common types used were Fordsons and David Browns. (Photo: Pat French Collection)

Although we were supposed to be on the strength of 172 Squadron (a Coastal Command squadron flying Wellingtons) us drivers were at the mercy of all the squadrons operating from the base. [29]

Armstrong Whitworth Whitley bombers flew from Chivenor in the anti-submarine role with 77 Squadron (Photo: Pat French Collection)

Vickers Wellingtons photographed at Chivenor. The Wellington was the main type used at Chivenor in the mid-to-late war years. During Don's time at Chivenor the Wellington Squadrons that operated from there included 172, 407, 547 and 612.   (Photo: Pat French Collection)

The Bristol Beaufighter long range twin-engines fighter was operated out of Chivenor by 272 and 404 Squadron during the period that Don served on the base. (Photo: Pat French Collection)

The Boeing B-17 "Flying Fortress" was operated out of Chivenor by No. 59 Squadron for a few months from December 1942 until the end of March 1943. (Photo: Pat French Collection).

Chivenor was a hive of industry. All the squadrons were involved with submarine spotting over the Bay of Biscay, as part of Coastal Command.

As I mentioned earlier, although looked upon as having been posted to 172 Squadron we were more of a dogsbody to all and sundry. Amongst the other duties we were called on to do were "flare-path duty" and "duty driver". Flare-path duty was an all-night affair, which entailed our laying out the lights down each side of the runway and being ready to ignite them at a moment's notice, then extinguish them after landing or when take-off operations had been completed. Duty driver was basically like being a taxi driver; a matter of "drive me there, wait and take me back". The operation was commonly done for flight crews due to take off, to take them to and from the operations room for briefing. At Chivenor the Ops room was situated in an old farm house a couple of miles out of camp, so it was a case of sitting in the canvas covered truck until the meeting was over then drive them directly back to their aircraft and usually waited until they had climbed aboard before returning to base.

On their return it was a case of meeting them at the aircraft and taking them up to the Ops room for interrogation, with the "powers that be" anxious to know of the situation during their spell over the Bay of Biscay. On the odd occasion a submarine could well have been spotted so, once reported, the wheels began to turn, maybe affecting the crews still airborne out there over the bay or the crew due to take off to do their tour of duty. Some of those crews were airborne for anything up to 10 hours.

I was told about an incident that had happened the year before I arrived. [30] Chivenor had an unscheduled visit from a German Junkers 88, which landed at the base during the early hours of the morning. It appears it was returning from a shipping attack in the Irish Sea and on its return mistook the North Devon coast for that of the French coast and having seen our flare path from some way back felt confident to land. From all accounts they were a young inexperienced crew so no sooner had they reached the end of the runway, were recognised by the duty ground crew who informed the duty officer, who in turn took them prisoner. Little did they realise they had done themselves a great favour.

On one occasion during morning parade the C.O. preached to us that our jobs were most important to the war effort but, as to be expected, we looked upon it as a load of clap-trap, and accepted our daily grind as a part of life. Not until later when we pieced together news from the radio and newspapers together with overheard conversations from aircrews relaxing in the pub, did we get the message.

Our convoys were being attacked by U-Boats with not only loss of valuable cargo, but merchant seamen. The situation came closer to home when our planes failed to return. Not only did they have success in sinking subs but some also came to a sticky end in the bargain. Some of the pilots were real daredevils.

One officer in particular I remember was Flying Officer Triggs [31] who stood out on parade dressed in his prominent blue Australian uniform. It was early in 1942 when he displayed great valour by returning to base on one engine, the other having fallen off into the Bay of Biscay. News of his approach in the crippled aircraft spread like wild fire around the base, everyone available turned out to witness him pull off a perfect three-point landing.

With the loss of planes and crews our attitude became more intense but with no sign of panic. Credit must go to the NCOs and Officers who kept our toes to the line, and making certain that orders were adhered to. This was the general routine during 1942, with everyone going about their duties with a certain display of confidence. From my point of view, I had one light hearted episode in July for it was my 21st birthday and was granted leave to celebrate.

I had to give full credit to Rita who made her way from Portsmouth to Birkenhead all on her lonesome. The party was well attended but spoilt to some degree by my flaking out drunk with mate Val Graham. You could hear us, as if in chorus, cry "Oh my God!! Never again." To some degree it was looked upon as funny, but by other people with a certain amount of disgust. Yes, we learnt our lesson.

Late in August of that year, having returned to Devon, Rita found time to visit me and having found accommodation in the nearby village of Braunton, we spent a pleasant week swimming in the sea at Saunton Beach. The beach was miles long and there was not a soul in sight. Behind us were the sand dunes which were out of bounds owing to land mines having been laid.

It was during this brief interlude that Rita brought up the point of her having to decide her future, for she had reached the age when she could be directed to help in the war effort and be drafted into an industry in an unknown town. She wasn't all that keen and had it in mind to join the Wrens. Both her dad and I were against it.

It was then I came up with the bright idea of her moving in with my family and finding a job to suit the purpose. She ended up accepting a job in Shell Oil Refinery in Ellesmere Port. I have the feeling she was jumping out of the frying pan into the fire, for the new type of employment was way out from the more sedate atmosphere she had been accustomed to. However, she tackled it with fervour and mucked in with her new-found mates.

Next time we met was New Year 1943 when I was on leave. Surrounded by family it was good to see her having become settled. But the trip home was to have unexpected consequences. It all started when my Brother Graham arrived home the day before I was due to report back. Graham was a Sergeant Air Gunner in Bomber Command. [32] I had not seen him in years and felt I should give him some time which meant I delayed my departure until the last minute. Then I missed a train connection at Taunton and spent all night in the freezing cold waiting room. Initially I thought I had escaped being an over-stayer as I was offered a form of recompense from my C.O. so I agreed to do a night guard on a plane fitted with new equipment. I was quite relieved.

Unfortunately, it didn't work out that way for the Guard Room Sergeant reported my offence directly to the station C.O. who was not at all sympathetic with my excuse of having missed the connection. I realised afterwards, I should have told him about my brother Graham having arrived home the previous day.

The outcome being, I was given 28 days at Chatham detention camp. I was not all that pleased. I was offered no amount of sympathy but that wasn't enough to have me feel any better, knowing what was waiting for me.

On Monday 4th January I was escorted by rail from Barnstaple to Paddington via Exeter and Reading. The journey was agony with all the changing and waiting, plus the discomfort of unwanted attention by other travellers. The trip by rail to Chatham wasn't that bad and I was soon on board the bus to the camp entrance. Once inside, I was informed as to where I was (as if I didn't know) and told I had to toe the line. No sooner had my escort signed me over, like a package being delivered, I was ordered to empty my pockets and sign for articles removed. It must have been near 9 p.m. and pitch-black outside when escorted to my billet. "That's your bed, down on the right-hand side," cried the corporal escort.

No sooner had I reached the bed than two airmen more or less pounced on me and proceeded to unpack my kit-bag, neatly folding the contents and placing them in the correct order in the locker above the bed. I just stood there amazed.

The reason for such procedure came to light a few days later when another poor sod arrived. The two airmen repeated the operation and this time I saw they were cleaning out the pockets for tobacco dust. This time they were lucky for later that evening I was to witness to what I deemed a most genius operation. The tools involved were a page out of the bible, a tooth brush and a razor blade. A portion of the page was cut out to form a cigarette paper that was rolled around the tobacco dust. The next part of the procedure had me baffled at first, for the two men were down on their knees between the beds and using the razor blade to shave strips from the handle of the tooth brush. The next I know; the shavings began to glow and the two were soon sharing a smoke!

The billet housed about 20 beds with a portion sectioned off to house the toilet. Emptying the pan was a daily chore taken in turn. Another chore shared by one and all was that of cleaning a rusty old cookhouse tin, left on the bed during the time the room was empty. The problem with this chore was the fact if it was not done to satisfaction it would be left on the bed and quite often accompanied by another in the same state. Our evenings were never boring, we always had some task to do. Amongst other things was keeping our kit clean the polishing of buttons on our dress uniform.

At 7 a.m. each morning we were ordered into the shower and supervised by one of the sergeants. Breakfast was at 8 a.m. with the meal being passed down from bed to bed until all were served. At 9 a.m. we vacated the billet, being counted as we passed the Scottish sergeant by way of a crack on the back of the head. Being January, it was freezing cold but this did not prevent the order to strip off to the waist and run around the parade ground. As soon as we stopped running, and were back in line, the order was given to do the usual exercises; arms and legs spread apart and touch toes. This exercise was followed by marching on the spot. From where we stood, we had a fantastic view of Chatham way down below. Once more dressed again and respectable we were dismissed and marched to a given destination; we RAF personnel ending up in a classroom where we could relax a little. The sergeant was an amiable type who encouraged us to explain how we came to be there and asked if we accepted the sentence dished out. Besides no feeling of embarrassment, we also found something to joke about. The arrangement helped retain some sort of equilibrium and saved us from going bonkers. As luck would have it I was awarded one-week remission for good behaviour. This meant my having to serve only three weeks instead of four.

On Friday 22nd I had to cope with that unholy journey back to Chivenor on my own, but at least had an inner feeling of content knowing the ordeal was over and done with. Like the journey to Chatham I arrived back at camp mid-evening and was welcomed to the cookhouse where I was served a meal of steak and chips. Unfortunately, such generosity led me to suffer from indigestion for days after.

I was soon back into the swing of things and enjoying the hard work. All went well up to Friday 26th March when, having completed my task of duty driver and winding my weary way up the hill to my billet off campus, I found it impossible to ride my bike up the steady climb so had to continue on foot. Not far from my digs I noticed the sky light up not that far ahead, so dashed into the billet, raised the alarm and dashed off to investigate. No more than a quarter of a mile up the road I noticed a large gap in the road-side hedge and saw a crashed plane ablaze with ammunition exploding. Then five of the crew, carrying their parachutes, went past on their way back to the aerodrome. One paused to inform me the pilot was one of the survivors and pointed out nearby two of his crew laid out dead. No sooner had I moved closer to the blazing aircraft than others arrived and one of them suggested we enter the plane and check to see if there were any other members of the crew still in there. Without any hesitation the two of us entered the blazing craft with him going aft while I ventured up to the cockpit. There didn't appear to be anybody on board, but having noticed the windscreen was smashed I felt it necessary to venture to the other side of the craft, where in the darkness, I found the body of the observer, also dead, and called out for assistance. Three or four bods dashed around to offer help so we were able to carry him around to a spot now lit by the blaze. We laid him out into a slight hollow where his face reflected the shimmering light of the fire. From where I stood it appeared ghostly owing to the fact only his face was visible, for his uniform and helmet being dark disappeared into the slight hollow. Then we heard the rescue party approaching and after waiting to give them information I drifted back to the billet. All went well until lying in bed with the lights out; it was then when staring up at the ceiling I saw nothing else but the face of the observer looking down at me. Such a ghostly image gave me the creeps and found it hard to drift off to sleep. [33]

The following week, Saturday April 3rd I turned up for work only to note everyone was on parade waiting to be transported to the town of Bideford for a street march to raise funds for the war effort. Having been duty driver the previous night I wasn't informed and was not dressed for such a parade. "Who is looking after the bowsers?" I questioned. "Harry Coles" came the reply. "That being the case," I added, "I will stay back and give him a hand." At that time, I was feeling relaxed owing to the fact I was due to go on leave the next day. Besides treating myself to a haircut at the camp barber I already had my leave pass, ration book and travel warrant.

Harry appreciated my offer to stay behind. "There's only a couple waiting," he muttered, "so if you do the one that just came in, I'll do that one waiting." While in the act of filling the one that had just arrived, another one touched down, but as Harry was first to become free he suggested I return to the office and he would join me there. The office was a small building linked by phone. It was situated up a rough track leaving the perimeter and proceeding on behind the hangers.

It was then it all happened. Not far up the winding track, with me feeling at ease, an image of the dead observer appeared out of nowhere staring at me. It was only a matter of 5-6 seconds but sufficient for my tractor to veer off up the bank of a bomb-dump and tip over on top of me. Immediately I was aware of being trapped under a weight of 25 cwt but still awake when Harry arrived. "God!!" he cried, "hold on until I get help. I'll get on the phone right away." It seemed a long time later when I heard voices again but unable to see anything. Then I heard the voice of someone superior, directing how the tractor should be moved, if only sufficiently to pull me out from underneath. Following the sounds of groaning accompanied by puffing and blowing, I felt someone pulling me out from under the tractor.

RAF Fordson Tractor

It was at that moment the camp doctor arrived from the sickbay, accompanied by the ambulance driver and Harry. Following a brief examination, he suggested I be sent to Barnstable Hospital "But I don't fancy his chances." he remarked. Still blind I was unable to see the expression on his face when he made the remark. Now with plenty of hands to assist I was lifted onto a stretcher and placed in the smaller ambulance and whisked off to the sick-bay and transferred into the larger vehicle. "Hang on there Ginger," muttered the driver who was an LAC; one of our crew on 172 Squadron. "I'll soon have you into the hospital."

It soon became obvious he had his foot down to the boards and in record time I was at the hospital and transferred to the x-ray room where they gave me every attention. "Sorry" someone muttered, "but there's nothing we can do for him. I suggest he be sent to the Army Hospital in Exminster." The next thing I know, I am laid out on the stretcher and placed on the floor. It appeared quite some time before I was lifted into another ambulance where I lay on the bed with what felt like a length of wood strapped down my right side. "Are you feeling comfortable?" said the soft voice of what sounded to be a young man. I gave my disapproval at being lashed to the wood but following his explanation I was prepared to put up with it. To add to the discomfort the ambulance was one of the old army types with a crash gearbox and every time the driver found it necessary to change gear I was would slide up and down on my so-called bed, with the length of wood taking its toll under my arm pit. Due to the fact I was still blind I was forced to imagine all that went on during the 45-mile trip to Exminster, but could just make out on arrival it was dark. They wasted no time in having me laid out on a bed, all done by way of torch, owing to the fact it was now lights out in the ward and the other patients close to sleep.

It was then I fell asleep and awoke late morning with my eyesight having returned to some degree and I saw Mum and Dad staring down at me. Also close by stood Rita. The fact they were stuck for words coincided with my being unable to answer if they did. Most of the conversation was conducted by Sister Turner, who was in charge of the ward. It appears Mum had made her feelings known about the state I was in, being still covered in dirt and oil and with the right leg of my trousers cut away up to the hip. I must have looked a right state. It was up to Sister Turner to offer an explanation to her satisfaction. I was then left in peace while they arranged accommodation in the lodge down by the entrance for my family. It was early afternoon when they all returned, accompanied by the hospital surgeon, who explained how treatment to my injuries was complicated by my having a crushed stomach and chest. "We have studied the x-rays which have revealed the right hip has been dislocated and fractured, the pelvis in the right groin area is also fractured, while the left hip is also fractured. We are now prepared to do what we can under the circumstances." A nod of approval was all I could manage, owing to the situation being hard to accept. "We will begin the operation at approx 4 o'clock this afternoon." Looking somewhat dismayed and at a loss to knowing what they could do, Mum, Dad and Rita made their way back to the lodge.

Following a jab of a needle I was almost asleep when I was carted down to the theatre and once the mask was placed over my nose and mouth, I was well and truly out of touch with the procedure. It was some time later when I awoke to the soft voices of two nurses. "Come on Don," they murmured, "it's all over now." In the dark surrounds it was difficult to bring them into focus so I was guided by their white collars. Both nurses stayed with me for quite some time, holding my hands and keeping me in touch with the outside world. Mum and Dad and Rita were standing by the bed for their words of comfort were also directed toward me. As already mentioned it was quite dark with torches once more guiding procedures.

Somewhere along the line I must have dozed off, for when I awoke to dawn's early light I became aware of both legs having been raised onto an aluminium contraption, through the knee of the right leg a large pin had been inserted, from which a cable had been attached and fed over a pulley to a large weight a matter of inches above the floor. "Oh my God!!" I moaned "what a conglomeration." It wasn't a pretty sight. A short time later I was informed this was to be my life-style for the next three months. It appears the time factor was a necessary a part of the operation. So be it, that was the situation and had to be accepted as such.

Two days later Mum, Dad and Rita returned home so I had no visitors to look forward to, but soon discovered I wasn't going to miss out when a woman who was visiting her husband in the next ward was only too keen to stop for a friendly chat. Other visitors also stopped to pay their respects. My new homestead was an army hospital which had taken over a wing of a mental institution. At nine o'clock each night the able-bodied patients were told to stand by their beds and once the Sergeant Major had made his inspection the order for lights out was given.

I mention this owing to the after lights out shenanigans, the time for joke telling. First one would raise a laugh followed close behind by another. The voices came from all areas of the ward, with the comedians recognised by their accents. At that time of night, we usually had two nurses on duty; one a very attractive nurse on the short side who wore scuff-type slippers and the sound of her scuff-scuff became common when she walked down the ward telling us to be quiet and go to sleep. On more than one occasion she and the other nurse would pass down the ward having told us off, and then out through the door to the next ward. We soon came to realise they were standing by the door listening to the next joke and were heard to burst out laughing as a result.

Every morning about 7.30, Paddy from the next bed was detailed to make the tea for all of us patients and he made a good job of it. He then assisted in dishing out breakfast. He was a well-built handsome fellow who endeavoured to appear authoritative.

At 9 o'clock all the patients (except me) were transported to a physio clinic in Exeter a few miles away. There they handled treadle machines and spinning wheels in order to get their limbs back into shape. In the quiet period to follow the nurses would go around tidying the beds and surrounds, which took all of a half-hour. It was then I became the object of their attention, having to be given a blanket bath which turned out to be something of a pantomime with soap and water being everywhere but where it should. It turned out to be a most entertaining half-hour.

When they had cleaned up the mess I was presented with a cup of tea and left in peace to cock my ear to the radio. To me, such a relaxing period of musical entertainment was like being in heaven with the door shut. The radio channel selected had all the top bands and vocalists of the day and, in the event I failed to sing all the lyrics I was up to humming the melody. The popular numbers I remember include Glen Miller with *In the Mood* and *Chattanooga Choo Choo*, Artie Shaw with *Begin the Beguine*, and the ever-popular Andrew Sisters with *Bei Mer Bist Du Schoen, Boogie Woogie Bugle Boy of Company 'B'* and *Rum and Coca-Cola*. Closer to home we had the ever-popular Vera Lynn with *White Cliffs of Dover*. Of all the songs to attract me, one appealed to me above all the others and that was a song revived in the film *Casablanca* starring Humphrey Bogart. The pianist Dooley Wilson did a fantastic job on his rendering of *As Time Goes By*. Both the lyrics and melody seemed to fit the occasion of our unstable wartime life-style and I can understand the reason for it was written for a Broadway Show in the 1930's during the Depression.

As Time Goes By

You must remember this
A kiss is just a kiss, a sigh is just a sigh
The fundamental things apply
   As Time Goes By

And when two lovers woo, they still say "I Love You"
on that you can rely, no matter what the future brings
   "As Time Goes By"
Moonlight and love songs never out of date
Hearts full of passion, jealousy and hate
Woman needs man and man must have his mate
That no one can deny
It's still the same old story -
A fight for Love and Glory
A case of Do or Die

The world will always welcome a lover
"As Time Goes By"

The more I heard this song the more I felt the closeness of our present way of life with that of the 30's depression. The one thing in common was having to fight for survival and live a normal life. Families were split up with sons and fathers having gone into the services in order to bring some sort of homeliness into their life they find the answer in visiting the local pub or a respectable dancehall and meeting up with the opposite sex. Nine cases out of ten such arrangements would be conducted with respect. But there again, as the lyrics go, such associations could become more serious. It only takes one of the partners to feel the strain and let their guard down. So be it, when two lovers meet, the fundamental things apply "As Time Goes By".

Following the musical interlude, lunch was served and I was then left to feel sorry for myself until 4 p.m. when the boys returned from Exeter. The noise alone was quite a relief but on the odd occasion I had three join me around my bed and using a tray as a table we played solo whist. The atmosphere was fantastic with one and all playing a part. We were aware we were all in the same boat to some degree and having to make the best of it. On the odd occasion I had a welcomed visit from Harry Coles who invariably had chocolate and cigarettes from the girls in the NAAFI. Now having been promoted to Despatch Rider he took advantage of using the bike.

It was about that time I had a visit from Sgt Steadman wanting information about how the accident happened. I hate to admit it, but like my failing to give the Station CO the truth about my being late back off leave and receiving 28 days at Chatham, I could not bring myself to tell him the truth about the ghostly image of the dead observer for fear of being ridiculed. "I can't explain much," I muttered, "at one moment I was manoeuvring down the winding lane with its potholes when all of a sudden realised my left front wheel was running up the side of a bank of a bomb dump, before you know it I was tipped off the tractor with it landing on top of me. Being trapped, there was nothing I could do, so I was thankful of Harry arriving when he did." "We have to admit you were lucky, Don and most shaken by the incident." "Just one of those things," I said with a half grin. 'It's now a case of time taking its course," he replied, "so hope all turns out well."

It was some time later I was informed of the enquiry regarding the crashed plane and how the airman who assisted me in the search blew his trumpet and received a medal into the bargain. [34] It was during that period in time, Mum and Rita paid a visit, staying a few days in the lodge. It was good to note their more relaxed attitude, which rubbed off onto me. It was a pity I couldn't get out of bed but settled for a brief moment of togetherness behind the curtain with Rita. The holding of hands meant a lot to me under the circumstances. Having now accepted a life of physical inactivity my spirits were suddenly raised for, out of the blue, Sister Turner informed me of the proposed visit of an orthopaedic specialist. He was due to visit the following week for I had reached the three months specified as part of the treatment.

On the Friday at 2 p.m. I came face to face with a specialist who was of German nationality, but this did nothing to detract from the respect in which he was held. The one thing of note was his bedside manner, he had a distinct lack of gentle expression and was most brusque in his manner. [35] He was accompanied by the hospital surgeon, Sister Turner and two senior nurses. During the quiet deliberation while awaiting his next move I felt like an actor playing a solo part in a Shakespeare play and being the centre of attention. Eventually he said, "Right, let's see the result of all this time and treatment." He then moved to my right side of the bed and suggested someone remove the heavy weight suspended on the cable. He lifted my right leg from its cradle and for a brief moment held it up with his right hand under the heel and his left hand at the back of the knee. It was then, without warning, he let the foot drop to the bed. My response was to cry out in pain and go through the roof. Sister Turner showed sympathy by the look on her face. Following a brief moment of silence, he spoke. "That looks most satisfactory and would now suggest you remove this pin from the knee and have the limb supported by way of a Thomas Splint. Following regular exercises on that contraption, it should not be long before he is on his feet and supported with crutches." Having uttered his medical findings, he moved on without as much a bye your leave.

Although it could have been looked upon as a snub I didn't accept it as such for owing to his expertise, I was now heading in a new direction hopefully towards a vast improvement.

The basic principle of the Thomas Splint was to have my right leg nestled onto a length of durable material with a hinge at the hip and knee. The simple apparatus enabled me, by way of two pulleys, to raise the leg as a whole then slowly lower the foot. The advantage of the two pulleys meant both the hip and leg were able to benefit from constant exercise. The treatment proved most efficient and before long the leg had reached the stage where Sister Turner suggested I sit on the side of the bed and place my feet on the floor. In a short space of time I was encouraged to stand and I was surprised and delighted at the outcome. Now filled with a renewed confidence I couldn't wait to continue with the exercises. By the end of the week I was presented with my crutches and now able to venture down the ward and chat with other patients.

At that time it was a warm, sunny summer, so it was arranged for some able-bodied person to wheel me down below, to bask in the sun on the spacious forecourt. So pleased were they in my vast improvement it wasn't long before I was transferred to the RAF Hospital at Wroughton, North Swindon.

Being an RAF rather than Army establishment it wasn't quite as severe as Exminster, but you still had to stand by your beds at 9 o'clock and be given a brief message from the Matron who was an RAF Officer. For all she endeavoured to assert some authority she was still approachable and easy to get along with.

RAF Wroughton, Don is standing in the back row on left in uniform. (Sutherland Family Collection)

The following weekend I was sent home on outstanding leave, from the time I had the accident. Still on crutches I found assistance readily available and so enjoyed a most comfortable journey. On arrival at Rock Ferry Station I was met by Rita. When arriving home, the atmosphere was most congenial with hugs and kisses.

Before bed time, Rita and I were managed a quiet interlude alone together and it was during the conversation the suggestion of becoming wed was raised by Rita and I did not hesitate but to agree. Under the circumstances, it was left to my beloved to take full control of proceedings. I might add, she wasted no time and with the assistance from my relatives, preparations were soon underway. It was left until I returned to Chivenor to approach Harry to be my best man. He became more excited than anyone and he soon spread the word of my upcoming wedding.

BACK IN HARNESS (OCT 1943 - FEB 1946)

Now back to the fold minus crutches, I was informed by Sgt Steadman that owing to my medical grading having been reduced to grade 4 I was now on permanent light duties and the boundaries of what tasks I could and could not do had been set. It turned out that in the weeks prior, an old vicarage had been taken over as a billet and housed about 4-5 drivers and cookhouse wallahs. It was now arranged for me to move in and take the responsibility of keeping the place clean and tidy. The old vicarage was up the hill out of camp and secluded by trees and shrubs. In the early stages I felt somewhat hemmed in but as time went on and my duties fell into place I began to appreciate the peace and quiet. More often than not, one or other of the billet occupants was present, especially the drivers or kitchen staff who had been on the late shift and had time off the following day. Having kitchen staff in the billet proved to be a godsend for quite often they would arrive home with meat in all forms; either steak, mince or sausages, not to mention tea, sugar and milk. Being experienced cooks, they were able to provide a substantial meal. It was like living "the life of Reilly" as my dad would say.

On a couple of occasions, Harry arranged for me to accompany him on a trip some miles out to a wireless site, with an operator who had the job of setting and changing the signal during the early hours. We bedded down for the night on stretchers suspended across the rear of a 30-cwt canvas covered Ford truck. We would bed down at about 10 p.m. following a meal of sandwiches of maybe beef or ham, plus a mug of tea provided by Harry who was in charge of the hot water equipment. Although not comfortable I enjoyed the experience.

Another new experience came along on Saturday 31st October 1943, the day of our wedding. The well-attended ceremony was blessed by fine weather, a bit overcast but most acceptable. From memory we had about 50 guests, all appearing to enjoy the function. The interior of the church, in which I had spent many an hour from the age of eight until the time of enrolment in the RAF, had an atmosphere that seemed to bless both Rita and I, while at the same time offering a warm welcome to our guests.

Don and Rita on their wedding day. (Sutherland Family Collection)

As arranged, the wedding breakfast was held in a large store in the town of Birkenhead and we were seated upstairs in the restaurant. When the lift door opened there was a chorus heralding *Isn't she beautiful.* Once seated and our meal was served it was time to cut the cake. To be quite honest, I was most impressed with such a centre piece, knowing how things were with war-time rationing. I was soon brought back down to earth with the knife in my hand when I was advised to stand back for a moment so the waitress could lift the beautiful object from its place of admiration and reveal the true piece of edible baking underneath.

Before… and after!

Thankfully, the guests were all aware of the deception beforehand!

Playing the part of a quick-change artist, Rita was soon ready for our journey to Blackpool. Following the chorus of best wishes we left the guests to enjoy the variety of liquid refreshment and beat a hasty retreat. For a surprise, when we reached Liverpool Central Station for the train to Blackpool, we were met by three or four of Rita's workmates who were there to give us a rousing send-off. With only minutes to spare we were soon seated in a carriage now full of couples who were also heading for Blackpool for the same reason.

To be quite honest, we were only too glad to arrive at the B.& B. and be able to sit back and relax. We were both ready for a good night's sleep. We never met any other guests until the morning and found them to be a most amiable bunch who created a jovial atmosphere. An older couple had a warm gentle nature and were only too keen to be of help when need be. It turned out to be something of a coincidence when we were introduced to the owner's daughter who was accompanied by her husband who like me, was also recovering from a lengthy spell in hospital. The other couple, from Scotland, were very bashful, they were last down to breakfast and they hardly spoke a word. All in all, I was quite happy and content with our new surroundings. As if to remind me I was still in the RAF we were forever face to face with airmen on parade outside our digs, or on the march in town. Blackpool, as I've already said, was a transit depot for airmen going overseas.

So much was there to be seen in this seaside resort, it was left to me to conduct our sightseeing tour around the town. Having made our way to the sea front and striding along the promenade to the busier areas we stopped to admire the Blackpool Tower, sitting atop the building underneath it. Apart from the magnificent Tower Ballroom there was the most eye-goggling aquarium giving you the feeling of being under the sea with the fish. One of the main attractions of the Tower Ballroom was the presence of the world-renowned Reginald Dixon playing his Wurlitzer organ. During our stay we were quite content to sit back with light refreshment and not only listen to him but admire his movement when handling such a complicated instrument.

As the saying goes, "all good things must come to an end", and in our case it had to be the honeymoon – the introduction to our life for the years to come.

On our return home, it was back to work for Rita at the Shell Oil Refinery, while I made my way back to Chivenor and 172 Squadron. November and December were, as to be expected, damp and cold which added to the slowing down of flying activity. It didn't really affect me as I was isolated from the daily routine of squadron duties. On the odd occasion when Harry was lounging around filling in free time following extra duty, I questioned him as to the situation back in camp and with a shrug of the shoulders replied. "Not much to say, it's a case of plodding on and filling in time as directed, but not neglecting the normal chores."

Plodding on became the normal routine until mid-January 1944 when our life was given a shake–up. Out of the blue, all of us (six male drivers) were informed we were soon to be posted elsewhere. In the days to follow we looked for further information for the reason for such a move but all probing resulted in negative results. We were sad to be bidding farewell to Barnstable and its warm countrified atmosphere. But before leaving we had one more night in town to remember. There were quite a number of Yankee soldiers in town but on the night in question for some unknown reason there was at least double the usual amount. It was a reasonably warm night; Harry Cole and I were enjoying the company in the local dance hall. Members of all services were present, including the Americans who with their female partners were the centre of attention; giving their version of the Boogie Woogie. Such were the antics involved; a female was seen openly displaying her state of undress when her flimsy frock was hiding her face and no doubt her blushes. While this was going on, the atmosphere in a pub a couple of doors away was far from friendly for an altercation had broken out between a few Yanks and some of our air crew. It appeared the Americans had refused entry to two black soldiers and were soon put in their place by the air crew. Within minutes the scuffle moved out into the street and moved along to the entrance of the dance hall where we were. It was soon to become every man for himself. Harry and I retreated into the toilet and climbed out through a small window into an alleyway and took off in the opposite direction and found refuge in a pub on the corner. There we escaped the Snowdrops (the Military Police).

At the end of January 1944, we were eventually on the move. On Thursday 27th we were posted to Northolt but only stayed there one night, for the following morning we were transferred to a Polish unit. They were awaiting our arrival. We were then transported by trucks to Hornchurch RAF Station.

No sooner were our feet on the ground than we were guided to our billet made up of two-tier beds and I didn't hesitate to select a top bunk. As to be expected, language was something of a problem but helped by two corporal interpreters, one of each nationality. They weren't perfect, but earned our respect. A friendship with the Poles soon developed with many of them keen to learn English, so all of a sudden, we had become tutors. My pupil was a middle-aged well-built man and easy to get along with. I have to admit he was quite keen. The Poles had a Squadron of renown at Northolt during the Battle of Britain, but this bunch of drivers had had no opportunity to learn the English language. The only two Polish words I managed to absorb and use quite often was "Dzien Dobry" pronounced Gen Dowbray meaning Good Morning. Good Night was "Dobranoc". At least I did learn something. As to be expected, with Poles on one side of the room and us on the other, it became natural to study the opposition and their customs and practices. From viewpoint on the top bunk, I soon became aware of more than one of them "titivating" their hair and covering it with a hair net before getting his head down for the night. I had to admit, such attention did result in a most presentable head of hair. They would not have learnt much from our lot in that respect for we all had the normal British "short-back-and-sides" haircuts. Their pidgin English become more understandable to us. Sometimes it was easier to understand them than my fellow countrymen, with any number of accents; be it broad Scottish, Geordie or someone from Birmingham.

By mid-week we came to realise the reason for our coming together. Our new 'operation' had us transported north to Manchester or Derby and return with an assortment of vehicles; including fire tenders, water wagon and ambulance. Included in the transport vehicles were 3 ton and 15cwt canvas-covered wagons plus a fuel tanker and mobile workshop.

Our first trip went without incident with me up front driving a four-seater Humber acting as chauffeur to the C.O, a Flying Officer who soon became very popular with the drivers owing to his liberal attitude and the attention he took to our care. On the return from our second trip north we were faced by snow and ice. The snow was inches deep and the ice affecting the operation of the windscreen wipers. It was suggested we proceed at a steady pace and at intervals, the drivers behind the wheel of an open vehicle would change places with one driving the large covered-in truck to get some benefit from the warmth of the engine in the cab. I was excluded from the arrangement owing to my medical ranking (grade four), but at one point I still agreed to travel in a three tonner with an uncovered cab with Harry Cole driving, which allowed one of the more unfortunates to drive the warm staff car for a while. One thing did have us wondering; all those vehicles we brought south were all gone within a couple of days. They had been despatched onward to unknown units.

For a break from routine, we arranged transport to Romford to visit the Palais-de-Dance. We were very impressed when entering the flashy looking dance hall, with the number of female partners to choose from. An impressive dance band added to the atmosphere. They played a good assortment of tunes and their timing was spot on. They were talented musicians. But all good things must come an end and it was soon time to have that *last dance with me* (a Waltz).
On exiting the dance-hall we were forced to bunch together to avoid getting separated in the "black out". We managed to locate the bus stop where we were informed we would have to change buses in order to get back to camp. The break in the journey turned out to be most convenient because of the adjacent fish and chip shop, of which we took full advantage. On advice I tried potato scallops for the first time, sliced potatoes dipped in batter then into the deep-fryer.

A month later, at the end of March and early April, we were separated from the Polish squad and posted to Red Hill. Goodness knows why, as there was next to nothing for us to do there. The orderly room seemed to be the only place on the camp that was kept busy. The orderly room was close to the main road, while our billet was way back up the hill. It was so isolated it made us feel we were in the middle of nowhere.

For about 6-7 weeks we were left clicking our heels and then without warning were on the move to Fontwell, near Chichester. Our new abode turned out to be a small wooded area with an adjacent open area. There were no buildings, our accommodation was in army-type "Bell" tents. Our first job on getting there was to dig a hole to serve as an ablution. The catering crew had arrived a day or two earlier and were fairly well established. The water wagon and generator we brought with us were well received; they made their jobs much easier. Our group was detailed to assist by peeling spuds and other necessities. Any other tasks were welcomed as a way to relieve boredom. The only building in sight was an isolated medium-sized brick house. I approached the woman resident and she helped us to do our laundry. She was most friendly and on more than one occasion invited me in for a cuppa. It didn't take long to become settled and accept what life had to offer, especially the novelty of camping out.

It was during a pleasant spell of weather we were to witness to a sight we will never forget, It was on Monday 5th June and approx 10.30 p.m. when we heard the drone of aircraft approaching from the area of Chichester. It got louder and louder and then they came into sight. The sky was literally filled with planes towing gliders. Some planes were towing two gliders at once. We were on double summer time, so it was still light enough to view the whole spectacle. We had witnessed similar sights when British and American bombers made their way to bomb Germany while escorted by fighter planes, but it was nothing in comparison to the scene we saw above. The warm-looking summer sky was now a background to what appeared to the long-awaited invasion of France. The spectacular sight did not need any explaining to us, and it was now obvious we were soon to follow! "Now's the time to get our feet wet." chuckled some smart Alec. "We won't be flying over there, we'll be walking."

But we stayed where we were for a few weeks. During that time, we came under attack by the latest German weapon, the "buzz-bomb". A small aircraft without a pilot packed with explosive. When the bomb was approaching you would hear it first; the distinct noise of the engine could be heard miles away. When it came in sight all one could do was to make for the nearest shelter or stand and watch its direction of flight, then wait for the engine to cut out. When that happened, it would fall from the sky like a stone and explode on impact. At night its exhaust flame stood out like a beacon.

Still in charge of the C.O.'s car, it was my duty to drive into Chichester each day to deliver and collect mail plus other incidentals as required. It was on one afternoon when returning from Chichester I caught sight of a buzz bomb coming towards me and I had to think fairly quickly as to my next move. The road ahead was dead straight with no sign of a turn off, so I could not veer off to avoid it. I took a gamble, a case of all or nothing, I put my foot down and went like a bat out of hell. I was relieved to see it sail past above me so eased off and took a deep breath. The incident didn't have a happy ending for I was informed later it had landed on the laundry in Chichester and people perished.[36]

Guided only by rumours we had some idea what was in the wind and expected to be sent to France any day. It didn't quite turn out that way. A few weeks later we were told to prepare for a trip to Salisbury for our vehicles to be water proofed. I once again missed out, owing my medical grading, for on the day prior to the move I was posted to RAF Tangmere Headquarters, a move I did not like. I had become settled with my present outfit and I was looking forward to going with them to France.

Tangmere Headquarters was a totally different kettle of fish to what I had become used to. It was run with textbook military discipline. For years now, I had worn wellington boots with submarine type thick woollen socks, the tops turned for convenience, necessary because of the often-unsavoury conditions underfoot. Now I was ordered to remove such uncouth footwear and step out in highly polished boots. Also, to rub the salt in, I was ordered to discard my battledress and replace it with my dress jacket and shining brass buttons, plus my peak cap. It was like joining up again. Having lived a lifestyle of easy-come easy-go for so long I saw my new C.O. and Flight Sergeant as my enemies. So, I was intent of making a move as soon as possible.

So be It! According to the Corporal in the orderly room my only way out was to be posted on a course somewhere and I was only too happy to co-operate. As luck would have it, just such an opportunity turned up the following week and the Corporal wasted no time going through the required paperwork. A week later I was on my way to Kirkham, near Preston. I was there to be trained for the job of storeman but they soon realised I wasn't suited to the job, but I was told to at least show willing. The tutors soon came to realise I wasn't the only one not up to standard. One had to have a photographic mind in order to remember all the information about each garment. It was amazing how many had men's underpants mixed up with WAAF's bloomers. Can you imagine the embarrassment when dishing out men's underpants to a WAAF wishing for knickers? Suffice to say, I wasn't the only dim one to fail.

For that period, I had been only one hour from home but unable to take advantage of the fact. Now I was on my way to Caistor in Lincolnshire, a base in the countryside far from a big city.

Caistor was a quiet Maintenance Unit (MU). There was little flying going on. Although the staff appeared busy they did not break into a sweat. I was lumbered with the responsibility of keeping the boilers going and making sure the station personnel did not go short of hot-water. I also found myself cleaning out the snooker room in the NAAFI and in doing so improved on my talent with the cue and chalk. I also found time to play draughts with a black African from Nigeria and found him a tough opponent. During that time a young airman from Cornwall arrived who claimed to be the junior billiards champion of the southern counties. Like the gentleman from Nigeria I found this young fellow hard to beat, but not impossible. I was only too keen to set the balls up for a game with him; for I did enjoy winning the odd game and gaining the respect by the billiard champion.

One day, for a change in routine I spent my lunch break in the NAAFI. I sat back assessing the room with mixed feelings, for seated at a nearby table were a bunch of moaners, bringing down the tone of the room. However, on the table to my right the atmosphere was entirely different with first one person making a hilarious remark only to have someone respond with similar joviality. My observations were suddenly disturbed by the background noise of instruments being tuned into the key of "C". It turned out to be the group of musicians who made up as the station dance band. I soon became aware all the instrumentalists were professionals in their own right. The leader, a Corporal trumpeter, played for a band in a night club in London. The violinist played for the Palm Court Orchestra and the pianist played for another dance-band band of renown. It was obvious from the start these musicians were not the type one would find busking on the street.

I don't know why, even to this day, but seeing there was no drummer I had the nerve to request I have a go on the drums and was accepted without hesitation. Maybe they thought I had some experience. My only experience was during the Christmas parties with my dad vamping on the piano and a close relation on his accordion while I endeavoured to beat out the timing on a Crawford's biscuit tin with drumsticks. Having been lubricated on an assortment of drinks, they all thought we were good.

When I was seated at the set of drums I soon realised why others had not volunteered. The base drum was one of the old military types, the pedal used for beating time was a bit floppy. The snare drum was again of the ancient military style with only one skin with a metal strip around the edge, which had to be avoided when stroking the wire brushes across the skin. At least the cymbal was serviceable! The concoction looked to have come out of the Ark. Endeavouring not distract from the music they were playing, I felt my way with trepidation. Using the wire brushes turned out to be my saviour, for I was able to beat out a tempo without creating to much of a distraction. I was amazed at my own handling of such a load of junk and was even more amazed to be praised for my effort. "One must admit" said the leader, "your timing is spot on." It then remembered how Dad and my relative made the same remark when I accompanied them on the biscuit tin. "Such talent as yours you have to be born with," said Dad "so thank your lucky stars."

Unfortunately, another good thing came to an end. Just when feeling established with the band, the leader took me to one side and told me I would have to vacate my position in favour of a new airman who had arrived with his own new set of drums." We are sorry it has come to this," he said "for we have come to appreciate your relaxed manner when performing. Although we have to accept the change we are not looking forward to it, for the new bloke is a crash bang type, who wants to be a showman type drummer with no respect for timing, which is what we really need." I accepted the situation and put his mind to ease. Obviously, I was disappointed but the look on his face as we shook hands was most rewarding.

To add to the sudden change of circumstances, a week or so later I was posted to Buckie, 50miles north of Aberdeen, nestled in a blanket of Scottish heather.

Buckie was a quaint town and although on the small side had plenty going for it, both picturesque views and entertainment. When posted to Buckie I was accompanied by a Scotsman from Airdrie and only ever addressed him as Jock. It was on our first visit to town we went to a coffee shop (close to the harbour) and was served with a hot scone covered in strawberry jam topped off with clotted cream, a delicacy we had never seen in years. Having mentioned the shortage of such items we were then informed of an office on the wharf that sold smoked haddock and delivered it to the door. Such a service was not to be sneezed at for not only was such an item hard to buy at home, but it was most convenient having it delivered.

We didn't seem to have been posted to RAF Buckie to do any particular job, so they made use of us by putting us in charge of a bunch of Italian Prisoners of War. I was also responsible for two conscientious objector prisoners at work on painting a mural on the NAAFI wall. Not only were they doing an excellent job, they were enjoying it. A few of the Italians made it plain they did not wish to be looked upon as prisoners, for they had lain down their arms early in the war and indicated they were not interested in Italy winning and criticized Mussolini, their premier at the time, for being pressured into it by Hitler. I was soon left in no doubt they weren't going to be any trouble as long as I did not apply too much pressure. I had little option anyway as there seemed no alternative. I was told I was the boss and to do as I thought fit. Within days I found out the Italians had become owners of a camp bicycle and spent much of their time in Buckie. Not only that but some had become attached to local lassies. A number of the young girls looked upon the Italians as being heaven sent and were only too happy to be wooed by them.

I was lucky to be relieved from the guard of the so-called "prisoners" when I was approached by an officer who asked me if I could handle a hammer and saw. He broke into a broad smile when I informed him I had served my time as a joiner. "You are just the man I've been looking for," he said, "I would like you to help the station maintenance man to brighten up the officers' mess." He led me to the officers' mess and described what he had in mind.

I arranged for the Italian prisoners to visit the local saw mill to bring back the pick of pine bark stripping; the outer coating shiny coat. We used it to cover the wall up to waist high and the surrounds of the bar window. Although a bit of a fiddle to handle we soon had it in place.

It was while tackling this job in the Officer's Mess that I saw a Flying Officer nursing his beer and knew right away he was the person I once had words with back at Gosport in which resulted me in taking a driver's course. Yes, it was none other than Sgt Rogers who was my senior on AACU in 1942. There was no doubt it was him and his returned glance showed he knew who I was. For all that we exchanged glances during the following three days, neither spoke a word of recognition. Maybe he felt a sense of guilt over the whole issue and had no wish to open up old wounds. I felt it best to just carry on as if he wasn't present.

About this time Jock suggested we had some sort of relaxation and asked my standard of ballroom dancing. "With a name like yours," he said, "one would've thought you may have had some sort of inkling about highland dancing." I then explained how my grandfather danced the Highland Fling and Sword Dance in various competitions in Scotland. "That being the case," chuckled Jock, "I will introduce you to our so-called ballroom dancing. I feel sure you will enjoy it."

On Saturday night, a warm placid sort of evening, we cycled the four-mile trip into Buckie and stopped to question the first person we felt could be of assistance. "Yer nay 'avter go far," said the middle-aged man, "it's just up there, up Church Street, on ther reet hand side. Yer canner miss it. Jus follow the other young un's, that's where they'll be heading ter night." Following his directions, we soon entered Church Street and wheeling the bike, walked up on the right-hand side. We had little trouble finding it for as explained; we weren't the only ones going that night.

Being strangers, we were approached by a young man dressed in a kilt, and guided to a group of people gathered in the corner of the dance hall. Within minutes we had been introduced and shook hands all around. They soon picked up on my accent and guessed that I was a stranger to Highland ballroom dancing, and they were keen to break me in. Given time to sit back and cast my eye over the strange surroundings I was then introduced to a young lass and informed she was to be my partner in the next dance. It turned out to be an Eightsome Reel. Having been introduced to the band; consisting of drums, fiddle, accordion and bagpipes, which had played a few bars of a number by way of a warm-up I was given brief instructions of what I was expected to do.

So be it! To start the dance, we formed a circle and holding hands we moved clockwise until informed by the band by pausing at the change of key. We stopped moving in a circle in order for a couple to move to the centre and with arms crossed they clasped hands and began to spin round. While they were revolving at speed, the rest of us beat time with a foot, clapped hands and encouraged them to go that much faster. Eventually they stopped and took their places in the circle. That was where the fun stopped, for the next thing I knew I was being dragged to the centre of the circle and put through my paces. The attractive young lady was no longer a lady, having a strong grip on my hands she was twirling me around like a top. Eventually my spinning head returned to normal and aware she was being egged on by those in the circle, so ended my first introduction to Highland Dancing.

To my relief, the next dance was Strip the Willow, with a much calmer movement but still lively When it came to the waltz and foxtrot I felt more relaxed and was beginning to enjoy myself. Overall, it turned out to be a most enjoyable evening once I felt at ease with the bunch of strangers. They were looking forward to our next visit.

Jock and I went on leave the following week. We found ourselves the subject of a statement repeated damn near hourly over the radio. The message announced that all those on leave when the peace treaty was signed ending the war in Europe, could extend their leave by one week. Not wishing to miss out I left all arrangements to return until the last moment, leaving home on the Monday evening and even deliberately missing a connection in both Liverpool and Preston. Still there was no sign of the announcement so I had no option but proceed back to Buckie. That was on Monday May 7th and, believe it or not, when I was at the gate of the camp about to book in, some bod came dashing over giving us the news that the war was over. "That's all I wanted" I cried out. "Why did they have to take so long?" Jock not having so far to travel, was already back on the camp.

During the course of the next couple of months personnel appeared to be in a daze with little instructions on what to do and no-one in any hurry to do anything anyway. The Italian prisoners had been rounded up and shipped to a camp. Wanting something to do and relieve the boredom Jock and I cycled out to Buckie and shed some excess energy at the dance, to which by this time we had become quite welcome. Whenever possible I would partner the young lady who broke me into the eightsome reel and proved to be more than a handful. She enjoyed it and always looked forward to the next encounter.

As mentioned earlier, our clocks were two hours in advance. Because of the extended light period we were able to enjoy the beautiful scenery and the purple heather in the glens when cycling back to camp.

As perhaps to be expected, it wasn't long before I was on the move once more. This time to Waltham North Grimsby where I joined a newly formed Maintenance Unit (MU). However, our work was spread over Lincolnshire the home for numerous bomber squadrons. The sites included Scampton, Market Rasen, Horncastle and Waddington. These were all in a stretch of English countryside as flat as a pancake, boring from the point of view of scenery. The only points of interest were found in the larger townships, especially Lincoln City.

The job was the big "clean up" after the war. Our daily routine included the search for bombs and other weapons to be stacked in a safe area until taken away by bomb disposal units. We sorted out furniture from the officers and sergeants mess, plus beds and bedding from the now empty airmen's billets and stacked it ready to be sold on. In some instances, repairs to a door or window had to be carried out and being handy with the tools I found it a change from all the "donkey work".

We fell into a routine, and found time to play a game of soccer most afternoons. Seven-a-side played for a whole hour. One thing which emerged from such a past-time was that I was fast regaining the form I was blessed with when at Gosport. All it now depended on was the understanding of other team mates, including setting up pre-arranged moves. From this point on things began to move that much faster and soon I was to be found in West Drayton, about the time America was putting the pressure on Japan by dropping the first atomic bomb. It did not bring about the desired result so they had to drop bomb number two. During this period of uncertainty, I was posted to RAF Downham Market in West Norfolk. I was now playing soccer on a regular basis. It was there I teamed up with Tom Buxsey, a happy-go-lucky type from Gosport. Of course, we had something in common with my having been posted there, plus the fact Rita was from that area. Tom, being a high standard soccer player was an asset to my improvement and I now enjoying the recognition I once had at Gosport as a player.

Following the dropping of the second atomic bomb, Japan finally surrendered on 15th September 1945 VJ Day. Like VE Day it was a time of let rip and do your own thing. We were transported by truck into Yarmouth and gathered at the entrance to the pier. There must have been about twenty of us, all without a clue as to what to next to get the festivities started. The surrounding area looked so quiet and docile, there didn't seem any opportunity to "let rip"! Eventually we decided to have a meal in the pier cafe and work something out while doing so. Many of our party had previous invitations to parties or knew someone in the area. So, after the meal people drifted off to their assignations. That left Tom and I on our Jack Jones (alone). For a time, we took just looked at the view from the pier then ambled off down to the beach. Some party!

On the way back from the beach, with the sea on one side and high-rise Victorian houses on the other we were still amazed just how quiet and placid the area was on such an occasion. "I don't know about you," I said "but being so thirsty I'm going to knock on a door ask for a drink of water." "Good God!!" Tom replied, with a half-smile, "it's like asking for an invite." "Not necessarily," I added, "I am really bone dry."

I chose a house that showed signs of some sort of celebration going on inside and as Tom had suspected we were invited in for a drink. It must have been at least two hours later, following drinks and food; that we thanked them for their generosity and departed. By that time, it was half-light so we found it none too easy to find our way around. We ended up at the station, which was deserted, and found a convenient carriage where we stretched out on a seat and eventually entered Noddy Land. "So Much for the End of the War!"

Following a good night's sleep, we were awoken by the slam of a door and the shrill of a whistle, followed by the sudden jerk of the train moving. "God!! Tom" I cried out, "I hope we're on the right train." "Not to worry," he muttered still half asleep, "we'll just plead ignorance at the other end." As luck would have it, we arrived at Norwich and when we explained the situation we were just told to move on.

"After the Lord Mayor's show, comes the muck-cart." The saying just about sums up the remainder of our war service. It felt like being in some sort of vacuum with one saying to oneself, "I'm still here, but what for?" The strange thing was that nobody decided to pack bags and go home! From my point of view life became a matter of regular soccer matches, home and away, plus being lectured on politics by the older men in the billet. In the years gone by I hadn't been old enough to vote. I was amazed how some individuals preferred Labour in favour of Winston and his Conservative Party, but there again, I had a lot to learn about politics.

One thing that helped break the monotony was my being selected to play football for an RAF team against the Army. The match was played at Kings Lynn. The tussle was somewhat one-sided owing to us RAF wallahs not having played together before, whereas the Army had played as a team on umpteen occasions and was also led by "10 Goal Payne", who scored 10 goals for Luton Vs. Bristol just pre-war. Although we were defeated 4 goals to 2 we weren't disgraced. It was a most enjoyable and friendly game followed by refreshments under the main stand.

Just prior to the dates of our discharge from the RAF being released, Tom Buxsey and I were summoned before the C.O. who suggested we sign on for another spell of service. If we agreed, we would be promoted on the spot. He smiled when we give him our answer!

So be It! Mid-February we were on our way; Tom travelling East and I was off up North to Preston, to RAF Kirkham Demob Centre. Later that day I was presented with my first civvy suit for over five years, plus underwear and foot wear. The following morning, I cried out "Good bye to you service wallahs." Armed with a travel warrant, ration card and back-pay I marched onto the platform of Preston Station, feeling if just released from prison. It was at that moment, I was pounced upon by a load of spivs who offered money for my new suit!

I WAS GLAD TO GET HOME OUT OF IT.

✝ ✝ ✝ ✝ ✝ ✝ ✝ ✝ ✝ ✝ ✝

SPECIFICATION OF AIRCRAFT MENTIONED IN THE TEXT

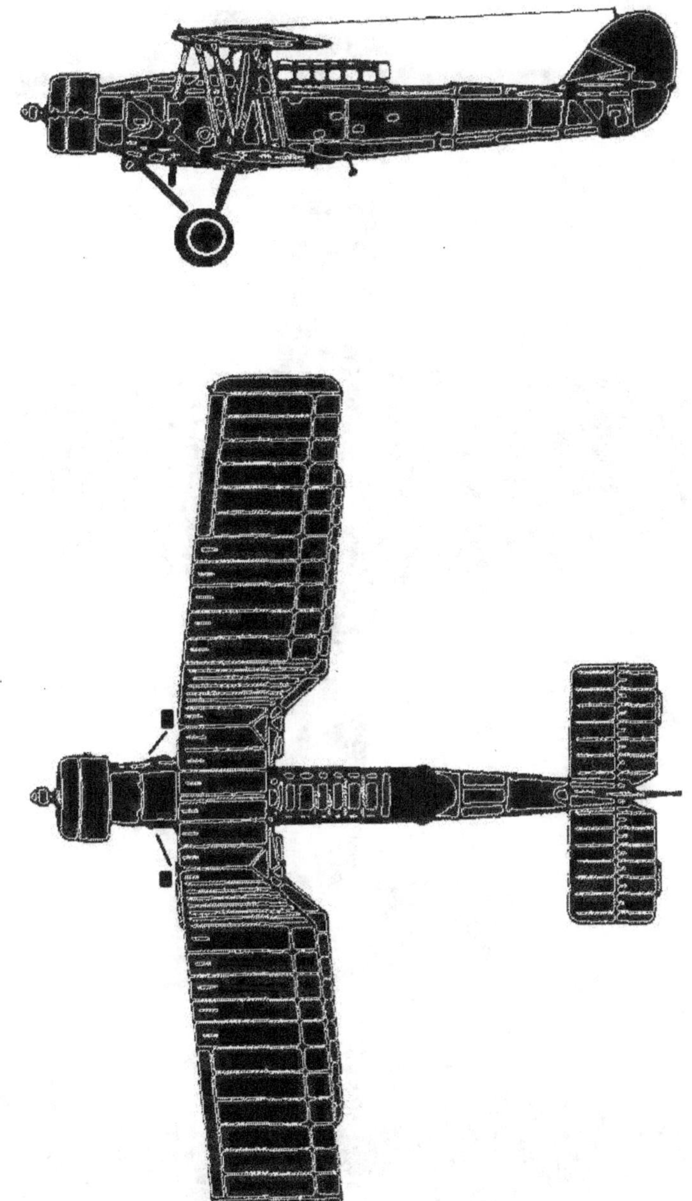

BLACKBURN SHARK MK II

British single engined biplane designed as a torpedo bomber and spotter to operate from aircraft carriers the Shark had an all-metal fuselage and later marks had enclosed cockpits.
Crew: 2 or 3   Top speed 150 mph
Engine: AW Tiger (marks I and II) Bristol Pegasus (mark III)
Armament, One forward firing machine gun, one flexible mounted machine gun in rear cockpit. One 1,500 lb torpedo or same weight of bombs.

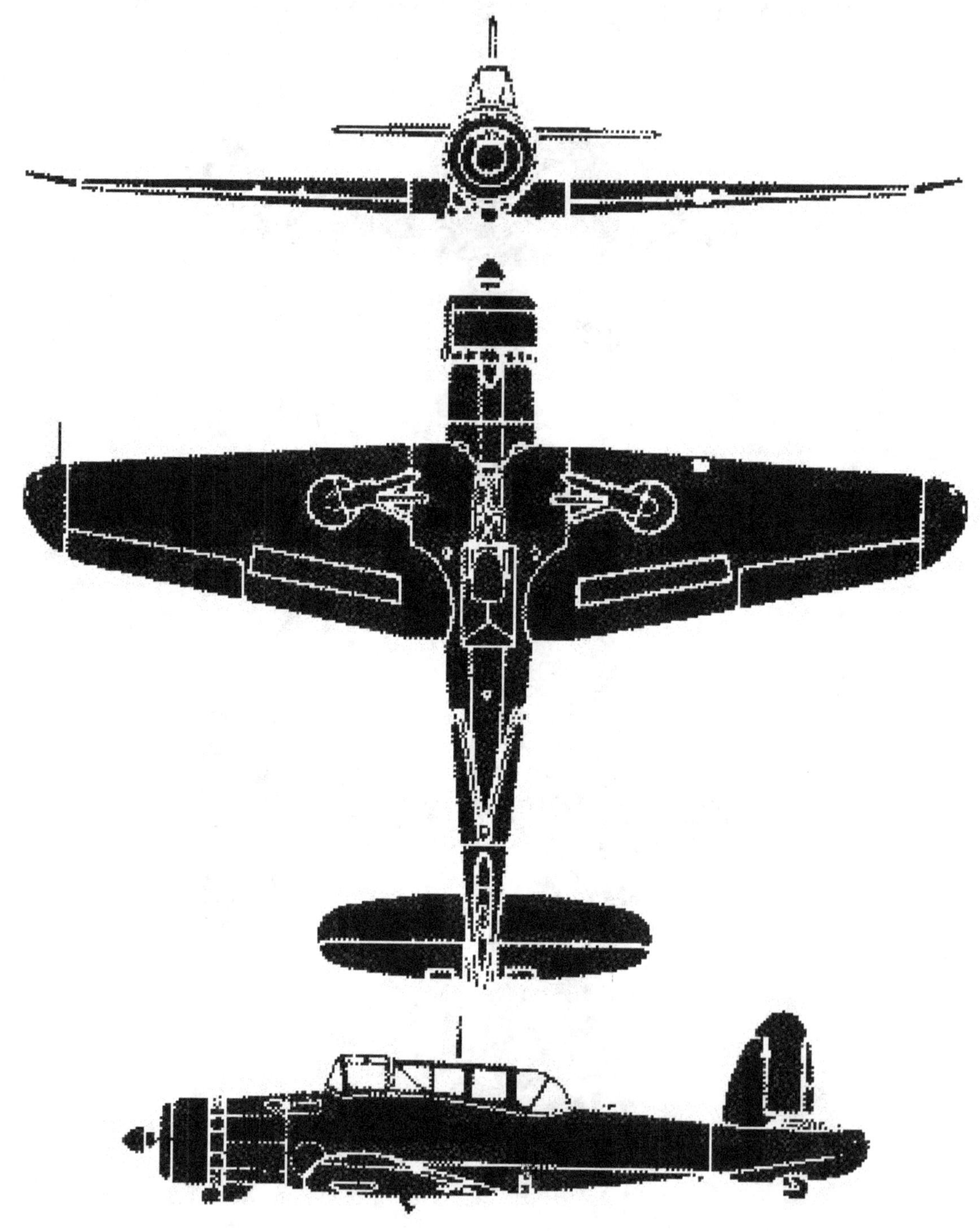

BLACKBURN SKUA MKII

British single engined dive-bomber and fighter designed to be used from aircraft carriers. Had an intensive combat career in the first 18 months of the war.

Crew: 2   Top speed: 225 mph

Engine: Bristol Pegasus   radial.

Armament: Four forward firing machine guns. In wings. One flexible mounted machine gun in rear cockpit. One 500 lb bomb under the fuselage and up to eight small 20 lb bombs under the wings.

JUNKERS JU87B "STUKA"

German single-engined dive-bomber used in the initial stages of the Battle of Britain to attack convoys in the English Channel, Radar stations and airfields near the coast.
Crew: 2   Top speed: 240 mph
Engine: Junkers Jumo 210 liquid cooled.
Armament: Two forward firing machine guns in the wings and one flexible mounted machine gun in the rear cockpit. One 500 lb bomb under the fuselage and up to four 110 lb bombs under the wings.

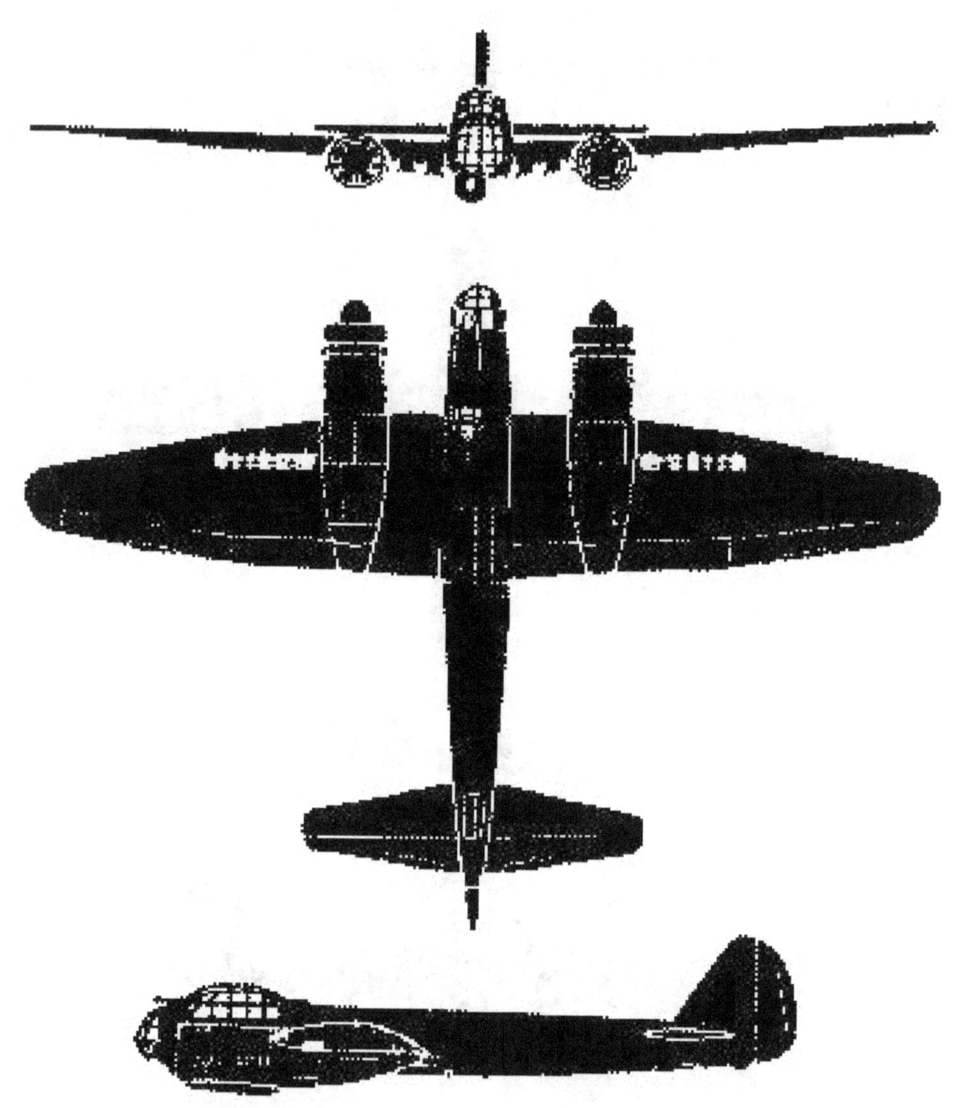

JUNKERS JU 88 A

German twin-engined bomber, the fastest of the German bombers during the Battle of Britain.
Crew: 4   Top speed: 292 mph
Engines: Two Junkers Jumo 211 liquid cooled engines with annular radiators.
Armament: Five defensive machine guns and up to 4,400 lb of bombs.

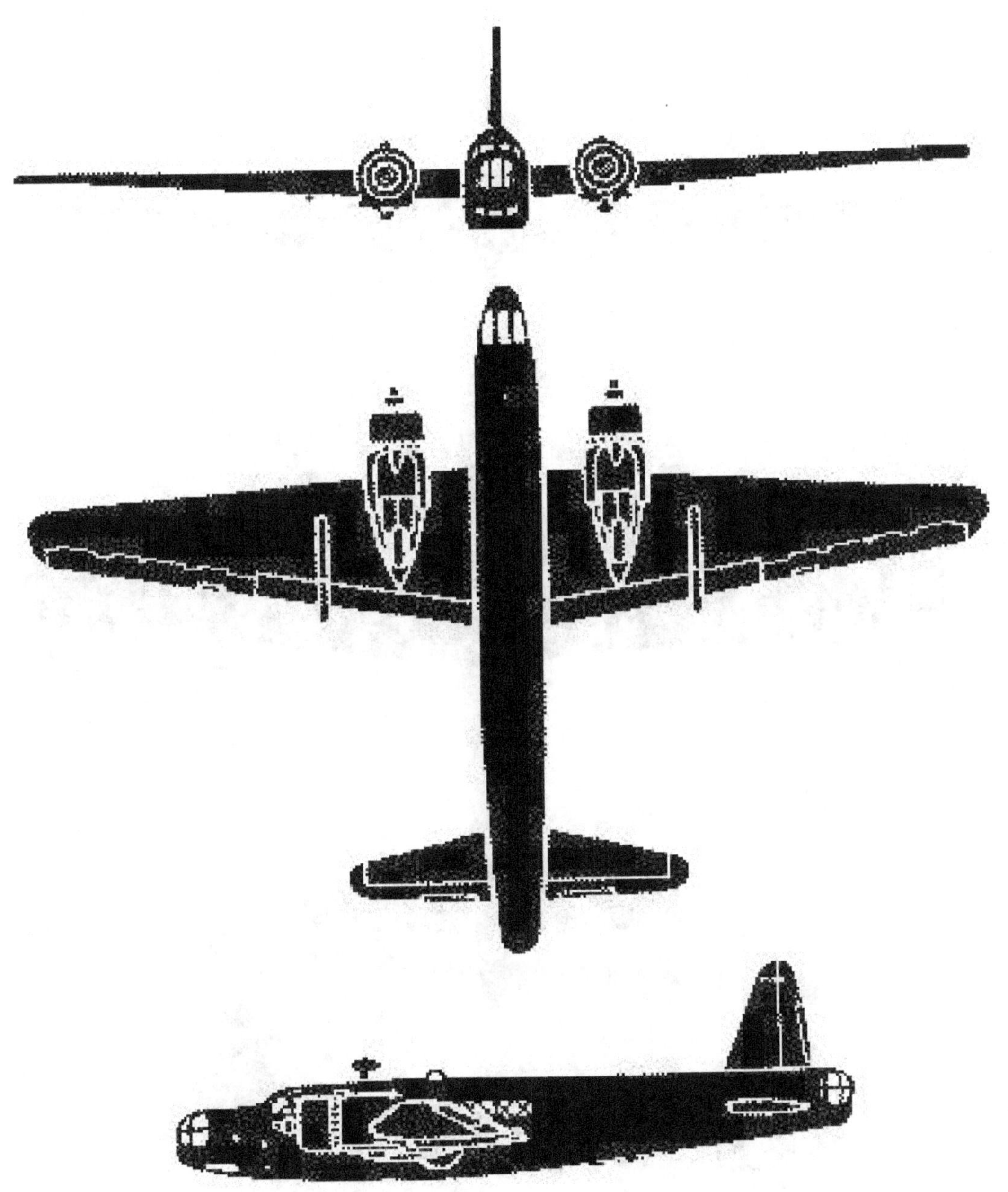

VICKERS WELLINGTON

British twin-engined bomber and maritime patrol aircraft. With search radar and "Leigh light" searchlights it was the Wellington that stopped German submarines transiting the Bay of Biscay at night, a major contribution to victory in the Battle of the Atlantic.

Crew: 6   Top Speed: 235 mph

Engines: Different marks used either the Bristol Pegasus or Hercules radials, Pratt & Whitney Twin Wasp radials or Rolls-Royce Merlin liquid-cooled engines.

Armament: Up to maximum of eight defensive machine guns and up to 4,500 lb of bombs.

BOEING B-17 "FLYING FORTRESS"

Famous American four engined bomber. The RAF used the early model "Fortress I" briefly in very small numbers as a bomber. Later the "Fortress II" was used in the anti-submarine role, again in small numbers.
Crew: 10   Top speed: 287 mph
Engines: Four Wright Cyclone radials.
Armament: Up to 13 defensive machine guns. In overload condition the Fortress could carry 17,600 lb of bombs but for longer range missions the normal bomb-load was only 4,000 lb.

ENDNOTES

[1] The Navy Army Air Force Institute, founded in 1920, provides bars and shops at British military bases.

[2] Vic Oliver was a popular radio comedian. Born in Austria he first found fame in the USA.

[3] Carroll Gibbons was an American pianist and dance-band leader who had great success in the UK.

[4] St Athan opened on 1st September 1938 and grew to be one of the largest RAF stations.

[5] HMS Thetis sank with 33 civilian dockyard workers and contractors aboard along with the 70 Royal Navy crew and overseeing offices. Only 4 men were able to escape. News of the sinking and recovery of the submarine dominated the newspapers and cinema newsreels that summer.

[6] In this case Number 2 AACU. There were a number of Anti-Aircraft Co-operation units around the country to provide practice targets for anti-aircraft guns. These were usually "drogue" targets towed some distance behind an aircraft but the units also used small unmanned target gliders released from a "mother" aircraft and also radio remotely controlled "Queen Bee" aircraft.

[7] Just why Don refers to his Shark as "1029" is a mystery. It is not Blackburn type number. Neither is it a serial number or works number allocated to any Shark aircraft. From his description of later events it is clear the aircraft he was looking after had the serial number K5651.

[8] Fort Rowner and the nearby Fort Grange are Victorian artillery forts originally designed to protect the Gosport Navy base. They were within the boundary of the RAF Gosport airbase.

[9] The National Defence Companies, a branch of the Territorial Army, were indeed made up of "old Soldiers". Aged between 45 and 60. They were used for static defence of sites of military and economic importance within the UK. They were later reorganised and renamed "Home Service Battalions".

[10] The winter of 1939/40 was extremely harsh in Western Europe with heavy snow falls and gales. The BEF (British Expeditionary Force) were the British forces in France, later to be largely evacuated via Dunkirk.

[11] Shark K5651 crashed near Kenilworth in Warwickshire on 5th February 1940.and the airframe was written off.

[12] D.H. "Nobby" Clarke, D.F.C. A.F.C. ended his Air Force career as a Squadron Leader. He was the author of a book "What Were They Like to Fly?" which detailed some of his wartime experiences. He also contributed articles to the Air Force Review magazine in the late 1950's and early 1960's that covered some of his adventures while flying with 2 AACU.

[13] The Skuas had been operating from the RAF base at Detling at night towing flares to illuminate any German E-boats trying to attack craft taking part in the Dunkirk evacuation.

[14] Boy entrants joined the Royal Air Force as early as their 15th Birthday and were trained in a very extreme, verging on brutal, regime. They therefore had considerable experience beyond their years.

[15] The Torpedo Development Unit was one of the units operating out of Gosport. One of its staff at the time was the novelist Nevil Shute Norway who was working on delivering torpedoes from "stand off" remotely controlled gliders.

[16] At this time, early in the war, the term "Radar" had not come into use, it was known as "R.D.F" (Radio Direction Finding) by those in the know. Its existence was not revealed to the public until 1942.

[17] The bombs must have been dropped on Monday 12th August when a force of 15 Ju 88 twin-engined bombers hit Ventnor with no less than 72 bombs. Although badly damaged the station was being repaired and some elements of it had got back into operation. On the following Friday (16th August) the station was hit again, (at the same time as Don was waiting at the Armoury and Gosport was raided) this time by five or six Ju 87 "Stuka" bombers which put the station out of order for two months. A mobile R.D.F. system was sent out to the Isle of Wight to "plug the gap". It was installed at Bembrige on the East of the Island; the equipment was on site by 20th August and operational by 23rd August.

[18] While the air raid sirens were sounded in major towns and cities in rural locations the air raid warning was often given by firing red "maroon" signal flares into the air.

[19] This attack on Sunday 18th August was part of an intensive effort by the German Luftwaffe that did extensive damage to British defences. The day has come to be known as "The Hardest Day". Gosport, Dons base, was heavily bombed that day.

[20] A drift is a tapering metal rod that is used to enlarge or align holes. Copper tools are used by armourers because they do not cause sparks when struck.

[21] They were extremely lucky not to set off the bombs, unless Don has missed out a stage in the defusing process carried out by either the officer or one of the armourers. The Germans used an electrical fuse on their bombs, rather than the mechanical type used by the RAF. At this stage in the war the Germans were not yet booby-trapping their bombs but still the first stage of defusing a bomb would be to discharge the fuse for which a special extracting tool had to be used. The fuse could become jammed if the bomb casing was distorted by hitting a hard surface and would have to be pried out with a copper chisel, which seems what to have happened in this case. The British were simply not prepared for unexploded bombs (UXBs) at the start of the war and the whole process of getting them to Ventnor and digging out the bombs seems very amateur and lackadaisical.

[22] A Junkers Ju88 was claimed just off Ventnor at 17.15 on 19th August 1940 by Sqdn Ldr A.V.R. Johnston of 602 Squadron. The Ju88 was the newest type of German bomber and most British aircraft recognition posters and books available in early 1940 either did not show it at all or gave a very inaccurate representation of it. It was often misreported as a Heinkel He 111.

[23] The attack by Ju87 Stukas on Gosport on the 16th August, the Day Don left to go to the Isle of Wight, had caused casualties and a great deal of damage. The repeat attack by Ju87 Stukas on the 18th did not cause any fatalities but many major buildings on the base were wrecked and numerous aircraft destroyed or damaged. After the Ju87 attack Messerschmitt

Bf109 fighters systematically bought down all the barrage balloon defences around Gosport which made many of the staff there think that further, even heavier, attacks were coming. Hence the amount of people on "unauthorised leave".

[24] Although there are known instances of bomb fuses being sabotaged, particularly later in the war, it would be almost impossible to fill a whole bomb with sand except under the most lax of supervision. However, the Germans did use bomb cases filled with sand for practice bombs and after the Battle of France they are known to have been short of real bombs. There are other reports of bombs filled with sand being dropped in the course of the Battle of Britain and it seems likely that Luftwaffe armourers filled up unused bomb racks with practice bombs knowing they would still cause disruption.

[25] Both Billy Cotton and Geraldo were popular dance band leaders.

[26] These so-called "oil bombs" were a type of German incendiary. The impact fuses fitted to them were unreliable and often did not ignite the oil inside the bomb, as in this case.

[27] To "do your nana" means losing your temper, going mad or crazy, as in "going bananas."

[28] In fact, the Nissan hut had first been designed and used in the First World War, but they were not widely used by the RAF until the start of the Second World War, when they became almost synonymous with RAF airfields.

[29] It was 172 Squadron that Don was nominally assigned to that pioneered the use of the Air-to-Surface radar and the Leigh light that made a huge impact on the war in the Atlantic. When Don first arrived at Chivenor there was also a single squadron (77) operating Whitleys. The Whitley squadron left at in October 1942 and during 1943 the number of Wellington squadrons operating out of Chivenor grew until at the peak of operations there were 4 Wellington squadrons based there. A squadron of long-range twin-engined Beaufighter fighters also operated from Chivenor (235 squadron replaced by 404 squadron in January 1943). The B-17 Fortress was another type operated briefly from Chivenor (by 59 Squadron).

[30] The incident happened on 26th November 1941.

[31] Flight Lieutenant Allen William Russell Triggs MBE, DFC of 172 Squadron. The following year (1943) his aircraft came down in the sea in the Bay of Biscay and he and his crew had to endure 6 days in a dinghy before being rescued. It was for his leadership during this event that he was awarded the MBE. He should not be confused with Flying Officer Lloyd Trigg, a New Zealander, a posthumous recipient of the Victoria Cross for an action flying a Liberator from West Africa which sank the German submarine U-468.

[32] Don's brother Sgt Robert Graham Sutherland was killed on the night of 25th March 1945, aged 21, when the Wellington Mk X (serial no NC555) of RAF 69 Squadron he was flying in came down in the town of Apeldoorn in the Netherlands (the town was still under German control). At the time 69 Squadron was part of the 2nd Tactical Air Force (2TAF) carrying out night reconnaissance over German lines.

[33] The aircraft that crashed was a B-17F "Flying Fortress" (known as a "Fortress II" by the RAF) of 59 Squadron, serial number FA698 Squadron code "V". There were 4 survivors from the crew and three fatalities. One of the crew (Sgt Clark) and an airman who was living in a cottage next to the crash site (Aircraftman Albert French) were both awarded the British

Empire Medal (BEM) for going into the burning wreckage and recovering the crew members before the aircraft burst into flames. This would explain why Don remembers seeing five live crewmen (presumably one of them was Aircraftman French helping the survivors downhill). Don's account would suggest they only succeeded in getting two of the three bodies clear of the aircraft.

[34] It would seem Don assumed the Airman who received the medal was one of those who turned up at the same time or after he did and helped him pull the last body from the wreckage. As mentioned in a previous footnote the airman who got the reward of the British Empire Medal was Aircraftman Albert French who happened to be billeted with his wife in a cottage right next to the crash site. He was therefore at the crashed aircraft before Don and the citation for the award specifically say he helped one of the survivors of the crew (Sgt Clerk who also got the award) pull crewmen from the wreckage.

[35] This was almost certainly Sir Ludwig Guttmann, celebrated founder of the Paralympics. A Jewish refugee from Nazi Germany. He established the National Spinal Injuries Centre at Stoke Mandeville Hospital.

[36] It has been impossible to find any record of a V1 flying bomb falling on a laundry in Chichester. However, on 11th May 1944, a month before D-Day, an American B-24 bomber that had been abandoned by its crew did crash into a laundry in Chichester killing two people. It seems likely that Don was told about this incident and somehow assumed it had been caused by "his" V1 bomb.

www.ingramcontent.com/pod-product-compliance
Lightning Source LLC
Chambersburg PA
CBHW080745120726
48001CB00009B/2696